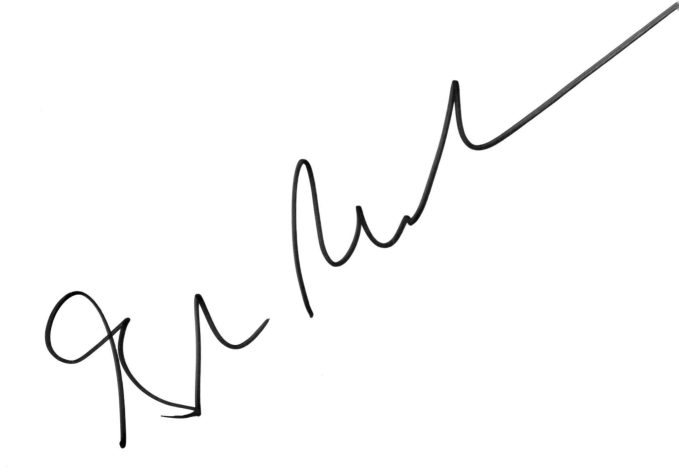

ALSO FROM CARMINE'S

*Carmine's Family-Style Cookbook*

# CARMINE'S™

## CELEBRATES

### CLASSIC ITALIAN RECIPES
### FOR EVERYDAY FEASTS

**Glenn Rolnick** with *Chris Peterson*

St. Martin's Press

New York

www.stmartins.com

Production manager: Adriana Coada

Library of Congress Cataloging-in-Publication Data is available upon request.

ISBN 978-1-250-04108-1 (hardcover)
ISBN 978-1-4668-3723-2 (e-book)

St. Martin's books may be purchased for educational, business, or promotional use. For information on bulk purchases, please contact Macmillan Corporate and Premium Sales Department at 1-800-221-7945, extension 5442, or write specialmarkets@macmillan.com.

First Edition: November 2014

10   9   8   7   6   5   4   3   2   1

*For Artie Cutler, a man who had a gift*
*for creating reasons to celebrate*

**—ALICE CUTLER**

# Contents

# Preface

Carmine's is the premier Italian restaurant in New York, the city with the most famous "Little Italy" in America, a place jam-packed with notable Italian restaurants. We stand out from those others because we serve superbly cooked classic Southern Italian dishes made to order with the freshest ingredients we can find. We serve our dishes in abundant, family-style portions that leave no guest hungry. We offer a wine list second to none, including impressive magnums of high-quality Montepulciano and Trebbiano, hundreds of labels, and our own house brand bottled in Italy. All in all, we seat, feed, and make millions of customers happy every year.

But Carmine's is much, much more than a restaurant. You have only to step through our doors to understand that. Carmine's is a larger-than-life place, where we consider it failure if someone walks out less than impressed with every aspect of the experience. Our mammoth portions delight the eyes and nose every bit as much as they do the tongue. It's food made for conversation and socializing. Our dining room is filled with the happy, boisterous noise of fun and people enjoying themselves, almost from the moment we open our doors.

Carmine's is the experience of participating in an ongoing celebration. It is the unbridled culinary joy inspired by the irresistible smells of melted mozzarella, sautéed garlic, and simmering tomatoes. It is the delightfully welcoming sight of warm dark oak gleaming in a pleasantly lit dining room, bejeweled with glistening glasses and shining brass worn silky smooth by the passage of a thousand happy hands. It is the exuberance and energetic bustle of the white-aproned waitstaff balancing armfuls of oversized platters of food on their way to a table of six or eight or ten. It's the ease they exhibit, weaving through the crowd and smiling as they deliver one stunningly delicious dish after another. It is the boisterous animated crowds at the tables smiling back at the unbelievable bounty they've ordered, not realizing quite what they were in for (and the delighted surprise as we neatly package up leftovers and send them out the door with another meal waiting to be enjoyed at home). It is the echoing laughter, of friends calling to one another, and the intimate clink of wineglasses consummating a toast. It is the simple feel of a starched white tablecloth under the fingertips and the comforting warmth of a

freshly served plate of pasta. It is friends and family and happiness. This is what Carmine's really is. Celebration captured in the experience of one of the best meals you'll ever enjoy.

It's been that way since the beginning. Carmine's owes its spirit of celebration to our founder Artie Cutler. The idea for a high-quality, family-style Italian restaurant got into his head after he attended a wonderfully simple Italian wedding. The reception included platters overflowing with traditional antipasti—basic, simple, and purely satisfying. Everyone was well fed and had a great time. It was like the Sunday afternoon dinners that Italian grandmas would cook back in the day.

Artie wanted to create a restaurant that captured that spirit, where people could experience a Sunday afternoon at grandma's house for any meal. So in the summer of 1990, he opened Carmine's. He envisioned a restaurant that was as much an event, as enjoyable an experience as anything on offer at the theaters in the neighborhood.

It wasn't about being stuffy or showy. Artie wasn't a fan of pretentious ritual. He liked to eat great food, spend time with fun people, and enjoy life. That's why Carmine's focuses on the fulfilling and charming recipes of Southern Italy, the most social of cuisines. To him, the bustle of a crowded restaurant was the promise of fun. That's part of why he started a whole group of restaurants—there's never too much fun in life. Artie loved life and loved to enjoy himself, and he wanted all the people around him to enjoy themselves too. That included the guests at his restaurants—first and foremost, the people that came to Carmine's.

Artie left us way too soon, and I'm far from the only one who misses him on a daily basis. But his spirit and love of life endures in the happy chaos that is the Carmine's dining room. It's not just the warm, homey ambience or the unparalleled portions and quality of the food. Artie was a visionary in the best sense of the word. His wife, Alice, took over the responsibility of running Artie's restaurants in his stead and she keeps his vision alive and the Carmine's celebration going.

Alice has made sure that all Carmine's

restaurants—from the flagship in Times Square, to Carmine's Upper West Side, the Atlantis in the Bahamas, the Tropicana in Atlantic City, the powerhouse in Washington, D.C., and our latest site at the Forum Shops, Las Vegas—maintain the tradition of abundant, delicious food, and an atmosphere full of friends, family, and the love of life that is Artie's legacy.

We had that legacy in mind when we were considering what focus our second cookbook should take. Our first, *Carmine's Family-Style Cookbook,* offered a wealth of the recipes that make our customers so happy. It is a wonderful book and was so well received that we had requests for more recipes, more information on classic Italian ingredients, and more of the Carmine's spirit. To answer those requests, we decided to write a new cookbook, offer-

ing even more great recipes and building on the idea of food as a celebration. We set out to expand on the information in the first cookbook, and we've done that with an "Italian Pantry" feature that I think you'll find delightful and a little bit more informative about where this unique cuisine comes from.

Just the same, our goal is still to help home cooks create the Carmine's experience of every meal as a celebration. There's no excuse for a dull dinner. If Artie Cutler were here, he'd tell you there's every reason to celebrate with your next meal—especially if you have your pick of Carmine's recipes. In that spirit, I hope you'll join me in raising a glass to Artie Cutler, Carmine's restaurants, and your next celebration. *Cin cin!*

—Jeffrey Bank
CEO of the Alicart Restaurant Group

& Sides

LASAGNA          28.50
PENNE ALLA VODKA    32.50
BOLOGNESE         31.50
                      29.50

15.50
14.50
16.50
NA    25.50     SHRIMP              SM 19.59
15.50       CLAMS
16.50
19.50                         9.50
                           16.00

Seafood

SHRIMP MARINARA
SHRIMP SCAMPI            35.50
SHRIMP PARMIGIANA     35.50
SHRIMP FRA DIAVOLO    36.50
SALMON OREGANATA     35.50
BROILED LOBSTER OREGANATA   P.A.
LOBSTER FRA DIAVOLO       P.A.
                           P.A.

CARMINE'S

CARMINE'S

# Introduction

Italians bring a unique passion to the art of living, a zest that makes every day a bit of an adventure and transforms Italian cooking into something more than sustenance. Long ago they perfected combining garden-fresh ingredients in compelling ways to turn a recipe as simple as a platter of vermicelli topped with an uncomplicated pomodoro sauce and meatballs into a dish that pleases the soul every bit as much as it delights the tongue. It's something that makes Italian cuisine far more than just comfort food—although it's the most comforting food on the planet. Each meal, each bite, is a tiny celebration of life— one that is meant to be shared with others.

That is exactly what Carmine's founder, Artie Cutler, set out to capture in the very first Carmine's restaurant. At the time, Artie had a single store, Murrays, supplying "appetizing" to the Upper West Side of New York City (the term is used uniquely in New York City, to describe a variety of smoked fish and related specialties). It was a small family operation, and Artie's wife Alice and daughter Jody would actually make deliveries ("We never had to use the delivery door," Alice explains. "The doorman couldn't resist a pretty young lady dropping off the package at the front desk.")

The business thrived, but Artie had grander ambitions. When a large space became available across the street from the store, he took the inevitable next step. The space was the front of the old Greystone Hall ballroom, which had been subdivided into a Chinese restaurant with several dining rooms. Artie saw it as the perfect home for an authentic "red sauce" Italian restaurant, something that just couldn't be found outside of downtown's Little Italy at that point in time. Fate smiled on them when they gutted the space for the new restaurant; they found fabulous period friezes along the top of the walls, and stunning architectural details including columns with pieces missing. The bones of the space fit the concept of the restaurant perfectly.

And so, the first Carmine's was born.

It was and is a noisy place. Alice recalls, "One critic compared it to eating on one of the runways at JFK." But the noise was part of the charm, a sign of the boisterous fun that Carmine's served up every night of the week. At first, there were chalkboards, a fixture that evolved into the menu boards Carmine's uses to this day. The experience of eating in the restaurant captured all the informal and welcoming charm of having dinner at Grandma's house.

That charm would serve as the hallmark, the unifying thread, of all the Carmine's that followed. As Alice explains, the overarching concept for the restaurants was Artie's brilliance. "Artie's great talent was—excuse the overused word—vision. He could see where the restaurant should go, and could visualize what the experience should be from the moment people walked through the door. He always said he was a businessman, not a restaurateur. He felt his job was to put the pieces together. He found the best chefs, paired them with the best managers, and hired waitstaff that understood the concept and knew how to put people at ease from the first moment they sat down." Artie knew that he had only to capture the feeling of a true Italian family Sunday dinner to be successful. He understood that Italians love to socialize and to share and value nothing so much as family and friends. Most of all, though, they love to share good food, wine, and conversation. Since long before the country's regions were unified into what we know as Italy, Italians have created meals that serve as a treasured way to bind family and friends together. It has always been true and remains true to this day: an Italian meal is a call to join one another at the table—the intoxicating smell of garlic, rosemary, basil, and olive oil an irresistible summons. Each new dish provides yet another reason to slow down, relax, and savor. That is Carmine's magic.

Artie had tapped into centuries-old and firmly established traditions. The social nature is what makes the food the centerpiece of so many special occasions. No Italian worthy of the title can imagine a wedding reception without overflowing platters of antipasti, or Christmas without the Feast of the Seven Fishes. How would you honor the saints on *sagre*, if not with a big bowl of agnolotti, a dish of Sicilian frittella, or the famous Grappa of Vento? Unthinkable.

But the more amazing aspect of the cooking is that it makes celebrations out of everyday meals. In fact, the indefinable quality that elevates Italian food to such a revered status around the world was perfected in the most modest kitchens throughout Southern Italy. The modern Italian cuisine so beloved by today's food critics and restaurant customers alike didn't really become what it is until late in the seventeenth century. It would be almost two more centuries before Americans would discover the delectable charms. In the meantime, all those delightful recipes were being cooked, refined, and passed on in struggling households all across Southern Italy.

Troubled by persistent poverty and a stubborn class system, the hearty souls that populated the ankle, heel, and toe of the "boot" turned to marvelous, sensuous cooking as the rare reason to celebrate otherwise

hardscrabble lives. Family recipes came to be considered treasure and legacy, handed down from generation to generation. Those precious time-tested dishes were the centerpieces of happy social occasions, the grist of pleasant memories in a world that could be a challenge. So it was only natural that when the masters of Southern Italian kitchens—mothers and grandmothers mostly—packed their bags for the greater promise of far-off America, they took little more than a few meager keepsakes, the unbridled happy spirit that is every Italian's birthright, and the most treasured possession of all—their recipes.

More than five million Italians immigrat-ed to the U.S. between 1875 and 1915, the vast majority from the south. They quickly em-braced their new home as a place of extraor-dinary opportunity and fresh beginnings. But the dearest traditions endure time and place, and for all that they would adopt of American culture, they cooked and ate as they had in the Old Country—dining as a celebration of life, family, and friends. The Italian restaurants of the time were modest establishments serving shadows of the cuisine; the only true Italian food was still made at home. And in those homes, the incredible care and fresh ingredi-ents used in preparing the food remained.

This is not to say the food was stuck in

time. Any cuisine evolves, and the Italian migration during the late nineteenth and early twentieth centuries was part of the cooking style's inevitable evolution from Italian to Italian-American. The Southern Italian tradition of serving noodles coated with a simple marinara sauce—far from ubiquitous in Italy, and even looked down upon in the North—would become commonplace throughout the immigrant's America. Some rituals and traditions were simply put in a new frame. That's how the leisurely family meals that were so much a fixture of life in the Old Country became "Sunday Dinner" in America.

Sunday dinners in Grandma's backyard were joyous feasts featuring the best family recipes, such as the "gravy" that was evolved from sugo di carne. Rich with expensive meat, this sauce was a treat reserved for the most hallowed day of the week and for special gatherings. Festive daylong Sunday meals included home-brewed wines, and all the relatives that could make the trip (not to mention copious friends and neighbors). These were happy occasions, opportunities to revel in one another's company and, perhaps most importantly, to celebrate life. The sun set slowly on those wonderful Sundays, reluctant to leave and miss any of the fun. Any lucky neighborhood guest was left wishing that he, too, had an Italian grandmother in the kitchen.

The special tradition of Sunday Dinner resonated with Artie Cutler, and it was a large part of what drew him to the idea of his own Italian restaurant in the first place. Artie grew up around many first-generation Italian-Americans, and their parents and grandparents who carried on the culinary traditions of the Old Country. He understood from a young age just how extraordinary authentic Italian (and especially Southern Italian) food really was, because he had the good fortune to sit at Grandma's table more than once. It all may have been very simple indeed, but it was magical, too, a blending of ingredients that somehow captured the indomitably joyous spirit of an entire people. So it was only natural that when Artie founded the flagship of his growing restaurant business, it would showcase his favorite food. He knew what he wanted on the menu, and that each dish had to include the freshest ingredients prepared in time-honored fashion. His restaurant would serve the same eye-popping abundant portions that made Sunday dinners so much fun (and were necessary to accommodate all the "surprise" drop-in guests that inevitably showed up, appetites in tow). But more than that, the restaurant had to capture the heart and soul of those memorable Sunday afternoon meals in Grandma's backyard. It would honor that tradition, and be fun and full of laughter with people enjoying one another's company. Artie insisted that it be a place where people could celebrate life with Italian food and drink in all their transcendent glory. That grand vision led to the birth of Carmine's, a restaurant that captured the best

of Italian Sunday dinners. To this day, Carmine's embraces the spirit and the culinary hallmarks of the cuisine.

Though all Italian cooking lends itself to celebration, it is the dishes of Southern Italy that most capture the Italian love of life and voracious appetites in equal measure. Southern Italian cooking isn't really one thing; it is defined by the particular identities of eight regions: Abruzzo, Molise, Campagnia, Puglia, Basilcata, Calabria, Sicily, and Sardinia. Each

contributes its own signature ingredients and dishes, but really, the similarities are greater than the differences. For instance, because all of Southern Italy shares an ideal growing climate, the food throughout the regions is marked by the vibrant colors and textures of fresh produce. For the same reason, the olive and tomato are king in the South, where they thrive in the climate. Olive oil is used in place of butter for sauces and searing, and tomatoes serve as the basis for many sauces and key

dishes. What began as a little-used sugo di pomodoro has become the beloved marinara. Slices of vine-ripened, sun-warmed tomatoes are the heart of incredibly simple and fulfilling dishes such as caprese.

Southerners also love their desserts, and what's not to love? A light-as-air vanilla panna cotta or a still-warm, sugar-dusted cannoli dipped in chocolate are nothing short of tongue-pleasing moments of joy.

However, as easy as it is to sing the praises of Southern Italian cooking, and as alluring as it might be to draw heavy black lines between Northern, Central, and Southern Italy, it's not quite that clear-cut. Recipes travel. So people from the North were always going to bring new foods and new dishes to the South and vice versa. Vibrant and continual trade is the beauty of any cuisine.

At Carmine's, we have always understood that Italian cooking is a living thing. It evolves over time and place, from cook to cook. The moment the first Italian immigrant prepared the first polpette—those delectable, savory, herb-rich meatballs—using Texas beef and purple basil grown in New Jersey, the cuisine continued its ongoing process of alteration and adaptation.

That's why we think of the fare we serve at Carmine's as Italian-American. But change though it might, the essence of Italian cooking—what makes it so special—remains the element of joyous celebration. It will always be a food for sharing with others, for creating indelible memories and honoring happy traditions. At Carmine's, we respect that heritage by cooking with the freshest, highest-quality ingredients we can find and with our famously large portions, meant to satisfy the festive, boisterous large groups that sit at our tables. We never lose sight of the fact that Italian cooking is the most social cuisine in the world, and it's about the people. Family-style *abbondanza* was key to feeding everyone who showed up for those Sunday Dinners in Grandma's backyard; nobody went home hungry and there was plenty of food left over for the rest of the week. We hold true to the tradition not only in our restaurants but also in this book. The recipes in the pages that follow are presented in our original, large "Family-Style" portions, but we've also provided strategies for breaking down recipes into smaller amounts if you absolutely have to—we'd prefer that instead, you invite a few more friends and family and make an occa-

sion out of dinner! We've also added straightforward advice on dealing with leftovers. No food refrigerates and keeps as well as Italian cooking, so one meal can easily turn into two or three.

Building on our earlier book, *Carmine's Family-Style Cookbook,* we've gathered even more of our best and most popular recipes. We've taken pains to represent the breadth and diversity of this wonderful cuisine, from the varied antipasti that launch many an Italian meal to the seafood, veal, and chicken dishes that serve as centerpiece main courses. However, just as Carmine's is more than a restaurant, this is more than a cookbook. Yes, you'll find mouthwatering favorites such as Crostini with Cannellini Bean Dip (page 22), Pasta Carbonara (page 104), and Mini Chocolate Cannoli (page 208). But you'll find much more as well.

This time around, we've included the stories of the classic ingredients that serve as the foundation for Italian cooking. You'll read fascinating backstories about basics such as olive oil and garlic, along with advice from our chefs on how to best shop for, use, and store these ingredients. We call it "building an Italian pantry." It's our way of helping you outfit your kitchen so that you can cook Italian as easily, enjoyably, and successfully as possible. Roast garlic and store it in advance, or use the ideal olive oil at the perfect temperature, and you make cooking memorable meals quick, easy, fun, and rewarding. As far

as we're concerned, the word "frustration" deserves no translation to Italian.

Building your own Italian pantry is, however, just one element of re-creating the Carmine's experience. It is the rare Italian (or Italian-American) Sunday Dinner that doesn't include a few bottles of wine. At Carmine's, we always believed that Italian food and conversation are perfect partners, and both are only made better by a glass or two of vino. Our customers seem to heartily agree. Finding the right wine for whatever you're serving is just part of the fun of cooking Italian. So we've included here an at-a-glance explanation of what you'll find in the Italian section of your local wine shop, and we offer a few more specific suggestions in the chapters that follow.

Whether you include wine with every course, or prefer a milder beverage to wash down what's on your plate, the food will hold its own. When it comes down to it, these are our recipes and our treasure. We offer them from our tables to yours, with the hope that you enjoy them as much as the visitors to Carmine's do every evening. Perhaps you can even start your own Sunday Dinner tradition, and celebrate in the spirit of every Italian grandmother.

## Celebrating with Italian Wines

*Artie Cutler knew that offering an authentic Italian meal meant offering authentic Italian wines. He and his wife Alice traveled to Italy and experienced the vinos of the Old World for themselves. It's actually where Carmine's practice of serving wine in jelly glasses rather than stemware comes from. As Alice explains, "In Italy, everywhere we went, the restaurants served wine in jelly glasses. It was part of the comfortable informality of the meals. I remember Artie telling me that the glass felt good in his hand, that it was just the perfect size and shape. We wanted to re-create that experience and feeling."*

*Artie also understood that the grape has always thrived in Italy. Italian winemaking dates back to ancient Rome, where many a cask was consumed in the wealthy—and not so wealthy—dining rooms throughout the empire. Even the poor in Rome would have wine with their dinner, and it has gone hand-in-hand with Italian food ever since.*

*Regional variations in both climate and winemaking techniques make for an astonishing diversity of offerings. You don't have to look hard to find an Italian wine well suited to any particular ingredient, dish, meal, or celebration. The trick lies in determining what's in the bottle, because Italian wines are often labeled not by the grape or blend, but by the region. Chianti is a perfect example. Chianti is an area of central Tuscany, but the wine of that name is made from the Sangiovese grape prevalent throughout Italy.*

*No worries, though; with the descriptions that follow, you should be able to find your way to a wine that thrills your palate and does justice to whatever you put on the table.*

### ITALIAN REDS

**Amarone:** Michelangelo faced the challenge of filling the Sistine Chapel's ceiling; winemakers have Amarone. The technique (known as *appasimento*) used to craft this wine is painstaking. It involves gathering a late harvest, and then drying the grapes before fermenting them. Many things can go awry in getting Amarone from the vine to the bottle. But when the process works, the result is beautiful. Rich with the heady flavors of dark cherries, plums, spices, and chocolate, this dry red offers medium acidity and a lovely full body. It is a high-quality choice, delicious by itself or paired with strongly flavored meat and pasta dishes.

**Barbera:** Not surprisingly, Barbera is one of Italy's most popular wines, thanks in large part to bright blackberry and raspberry flavors that are sharpened by an acidic nature. The wine is said to "pop" in the mouth, bursting with flavor and character. Serve it as a crowd-pleaser at a cocktail party, or match the medium body and scintillating tones to marinara or meat sauces.

ries, eucalyptus, and truffles all captured in a sturdy body. The wine named for the grape itself offers the flavors of dried cherries, leather, licorice, and violet. All of these are best paired with strong, hearty flavors including beef and rich tomato sauces.

**Chianti:** Say "Chianti" and most people picture a squat, round, straw-covered bottle. Chianti's stubborn reputation as "just a table red" doesn't reflect the high quality of today's offerings. The wine is considered bold and fruity, with a medium body and a bright, tart cherry flavor. It is best served with richer dishes.

**Nero d'Avola**: This is the crown jewel grape of Sicily's winemakers, and the medium-big wine it produces features the ripe, well-rounded flavors of cooked plum and pepper. It's a lot like a Syrah or Shiraz.

**Montepulciano d'Abruzzo:** An inky dark color makes this "rustic" wine a beauty in the glass, while the hints of black cherry, figs, and the low acidity make it a treat on the tongue and perfect for pairing with main courses of all kinds.

**Brunello di Montalcino:** Made of Sangiovese Grosso grapes, Brunello is traditionally aged for a significant period in oak casks, giving it a complex flavor and character. It is a big, "meaty," strong wine with flavors of blue-

**Barbaresco, Barolo, and Nebbiolo:** Named for the Italian word for "fog," the Nebbiolo grape of the Piedmont region produces full-bodied, lightly colored wines. The wines are "big" when young, but at their best when allowed to age, so that the flavors and tannin blend and balance. Barbaresco features a more "feminine" nature that includes floral notes and a lovely sweet perfume, as well as delicate spice tones. Barolo, on the other hand, tends toward the "masculine," with assertive flavors that can include chocolate, leather, mint, ber-

berry, chocolate, and pepper. The wine pairs well with meats and strongly flavored dishes of all kinds.

**Pinot Nero:** The Italian name for the Pinot Noir grape, Pinot Nero wines are fruity, understated, and light. The grape is somewhat difficult to grow, but a good bottle can make for an excellent complement to light appetizers or cheese and bread.

**Dolcetto:** Although the name translates to "little sweet one," the wine itself is dry, light-to medium-bodied, and flavored with hints of plum, prune, black cherry, and licorice. The acidity is generally low, and the wine drinks well alone, or paired with pork or leaner meat, and pastas in tomato sauces.

**Negro Amaro:** The name translates to "black" and "bitter" and at least the first part is true. This wine is the color of ink, and is complex, big, and powerful. It has a strong aroma, earth tones, and the flavors of ground spices including cinnamon and cloves, as well as slightly earthy flavors.

**Sagrantino:** A big, bold wine, Sagrantino is produced exclusively within Italy's borders. It is dense, heavy and thick with the flavors of dark berries, smoke, and minerals. The wine is one of the most tannic Italian wines, a feature undercut by the grape's natural modest sweetness. This is a wine for a heavy meal, full of aggressive, meaty flavors. It is better with dishes that are rich in olive oil, fats, and tomato rather than those that are cream- or butter-based.

**Aglianico:** Another big wine, Aglianico requires a bit of aging to mellow, but when given time, it offers a full body and wonderfully rounded flavors of chocolate and plum. Its high acidity begs to be partnered with fat-marbled meat, or naturally richer meats like lamb.

**Super Tuscans:** Skirting the rules, Italian winemakers sought to blend Sangiovese grapes with Cabernet, Merlot, Cabernet Franc, or Syrah. The results were rich, dense wines with the flavors of dark berry fruit, and a pronounced earthy character. The wines remain special—with prices that reflect their obvious high quality.

## ITALIAN WHITES

Age is the enemy of most Italian white wines. When buying a bottle of one of these, look for a date as close as possible to the current vintage.

**Pinot Grigio:** A justly famous light white full of fruit tones—including melon, lemon, and apple—this is the Italian clone of the French Pinot Gris. The wine is named for the grape and has a bright acidity with modest "greenness" that makes it ideal for summer meals on the patio. It is also great for pairing with lighter antipasti at a party.

**Soave:** Produced from the odd-sounding Garganega grape, Soave has a light to medium body and rich floral and fruit flavors that bring to mind honeysuckle and pineapple. It's a great white to start off a multicourse meal, or to serve with appetizers such as bruschetta. It also pairs well with seafood and lighter pasta dishes.

**Gavi:** Also labeled "Gavi di Gavi" and "Cortese di Gavi," this excellent white features a light to medium body, and is renowned for its silky texture. The wine contains a sophisticated and complex mix of flavors, most notably, ripe pear. It goes wonderfully with fish, veal, pork, and pasta in white sauce.

**Vernaccia:** Vernaccia is a grape grown in Tuscany, with a long and noble history that dates back more than seven centuries. Physically beautiful, with a lovely golden color, the wine is strong and full-bodied. It offers a dry, crisp, and complex mix of flavors with a pronounced bite of acid and a bit of mineral flavor. It can stand up to full-flavored main courses.

**Falanghina:** Originally imported from Greece and now typically grown in Campania, this ancient grape creates a light-bodied wine with the flavors of nectarine and orange blossoms, and subtle hints of almond. It is most famously served with seafood—especially shellfish.

**Fiano:** The grape produces a fresh, crisp, vibrant wine with hints of smoke, nuts, citrus, and honey. It is well-balanced and ideal for pairing with salads, lighter seafood, and vegetable pastas.

**Vermentino:** This straw-colored wine has a light to medium body with a bright, light character. It is distinguished by the bite of acid and floral notes with just a hint of mineral. Consider partnering Vermentino with chicken or seafood in cream sauces, or plain seafood of all types.

## ITALIAN SPARKLING WINES

Leave it to the Italians to invent two versions of this most celebratory of wines. Italian bubbly can be either spumante ("sparkling") or frizzante ("fizzing" or "foaming"). True Italian spumantes will be nearly as effervescent as Champagne or other traditional sparkling wines. Frizzante wines have more subdued carbonation that just barely tickles the tongue.

**Prosecco:** Prosecco is a lovely Champagne alternative that is dry and lean, with a bit more fruit flavors than other Italian sparkling wines. It goes wonderfully with dishes such as risotto and shellfish, served as a cocktail mixed with fruit juices, or alone as an aperitif. Due to the way Prosecco is made, it is rarely aged more than a few months—meaning even extremely good bottles are inexpensive.

**Franciacorta:** Made from a combination of Chardonnay, Pinot Nero, and Pinot Blanco grapes, this bubbly is considered Italy's Champagne. Technically, though, it is the best example of an Italian spumante. It's dry, with a light to medium body that is perfect for pairing with shrimp or lighter fish, or even seafood pasta. It's also a wonderful special-occasion wine all by itself.

**Moscato d'Asti:** Like all Astis, this wine is crafted in the Asti region of Piedmont, from the Moscato grape. It is a true frizzante wine, lightly sweet, with hints of fresh peaches and apricots. It is considered a dessert wine, but would be equally good with a simple plate of aged cheeses.

**Lambrusco:** This semisweet to dry wine produces soft bubbles that barely tickle the tongue, with satisfyingly complex berry flavors and a modest acidic bite. Drink drier versions with main-course pastas in hearty red sauces, saving sweeter styles for appetizer courses that feature cured meats, or for pre-dinner cocktails.

**Brachetto d'Acqui:** An enchanting, frothy and lightly sweet rosé, this frizzante wine features a strong aroma, heavy with raspberries and strawberries and hints of rose petals. It is a terrific dessert wine.

## SPEAKING ITALIAN

As you might expect, you'll see a lot of foreign terms on the label of a bottle of Italian wine. Some are specific, and others are less so, but all tell a story about whats inside.

**Vino da Tavola:** This translates directly to "Wine of the Table," and is the term used on any wine that does not follow the rules of the region—the wine can be made from any varietal in any way. These are typically simple wines representing good values. Most Italian table wines are delicious and eminently drinkable.

**IGT (Indicazione Geografica Tipica/Indication of Typical Geography):** These wines use the typical grapes grown in the region, but do not follow the winemaking rules and often include different or nontraditional varietals, and are not a traditional style. There are many very expensive wines in this category, such as the Super Tuscans.

**DOC (Denominazione do Origine Controllata/ Denomination of Controlled Origin):** the wine is made with specific grapes and the vinification and aging are done within very specific requirements outlined in law.

**DOCG (Denominazione do Origine Controllata e Garantita /Denomination of Controlled Origin and Guarantee):** One step above DOC and the highest designation an Italian wine can be given, it means the wine is DOC and must pass a blind tasting, in addition to stringently following winemaking laws.

**Riserva:** It's a fancy-sounding term that basically means the wine in the bottle was aged longer than wines of that type normally are. This typically denotes higher quality (although not always), and universally adds to the price tag of the wine.

## PAIRING ITALIAN WINES

The rules of Italian wine, like Italian traffic laws, beg to be broken. However, it's wise to know the rules for matching the wine to food before you start to circumvent them. Play it safe by matching milder foods—those that go light on the spices and fat—to mild wines. In

the same vein, match dishes with bold flavors and flavor combinations to bigger and bolder wines. Rich sauces call for a rich wine, where lean foods like simple bruschetta or vegetable appetizers demand a lean wine. Like goes with like.

That's why even though it might seem like too much, use an acidic wine with an acidic sauce like a tomato-based ragu. Use a wine with a lot of tannin or acid to cut naturally richer foods—but not foods made rich by cream or butter. If there are a lot of hot spices in the dish, consider pairing it with a slightly sweeter or fruitier wine.

It makes sense when you think about it. A lot of acid or flavor can overwhelm a leaner, simpler wine. You want the wine to complement and hold its own against the food without overpowering the flavors in the dish. That said, there's lot of room for personal preference in pairing.

# Cold Appetizers

Marinated Button
   Mushrooms   20

Crostini with Cannellini
   Bean Dip   22

Cured Salmon with Lemon
   Mascarpone   26

Rolled Beef with Hot Cherry
   Peppers   28

Naples-Style Cauliflower with
   Lemon and Anchovy
   Vinaigrette   31

Grilled Shrimp with Fennel   32

Orzo and Fresh Tuna Salad   35

Farro with Wild Mushrooms   36

Cubanelle Peppers Stuffed
   with Three Cheeses   38

Roasted Eggplant Dip   40

Romano and Black Pepper
   Bread Sticks   41

Literally translated, *antipasti* means "before the meal" (and it's the plural of antipasto). It's a simple word but a complex idea. This course most likely began when Italian workingmen arrived home after a long day in the hot sun. Dinner would still be cooking, so the hungry soul—tempted by the aromas filling the kitchen—would sit, relax, and take the edge off his hunger with a simple snack of a little bread, cheese, salami, or other finger food. It proved to be a civilized way to glide into the main course. From that humble beginning came a full-blown ritual that now includes an incredible selection of recipes that can be mixed and matched to create a wholly original beginning to your meal.

Traditionally, antipasti were served on a central platter, with each person at the table given a small saucer for their own selections. They were meant to be true family style—meal starters, and were right in keeping with the idea of food as social centerpiece in the Italian home. Understandably, these platters found their way into special occasions, and Italian wedding receptions to this day are sure to start with a few platters of these wonderful dishes.

These days, home cooks and hosts have expanded on the notion, often serving antipasti in the manner of hors d'oeuvre or Spanish tapas. That adaptability is one of the most alluring aspects of these recipes; antipasti can fill just about any role for any occasion. Use them as wonderful shared appetizers that set the stage for your main course, or choose an inspired selection to bring a memorable culinary experience to a special event. You can even liven up a cocktail party with a couple trays of these simple, flavor-packed creations.

The cold versions in this chapter are natural choices for sparkling al fresco meals on warm spring or summer days. They present such a variety of flavors that they beg to be served with a glass of something that will help wake up the palate. A little sparkling wine such as Prosecco or Franciacorta is perfect, as is a crisp bright, lively white wine like Soave, Pinot Grigio, Vernaccia, or Vermentino. You could even serve these with a lighter red such as Pinot Nero.

No matter how and when you serve them, the underlying idea behind antipasti remains the same. Each simple recipe focuses on one main flavor or ingredient, which the

ing the individual dishes into a presentation that is greater than the sum of its parts. A thoughtfully selected antipasti platter is a choreography of food textures, flavors, forms, and colors. There should always be something for the eye, the teeth, and the tongue. The flavors, too, must work in concert. Not only should they complement one another—none too similar, nor jarringly different—they must also do justice to the flavors of the main course. Ideally, the antipasti manages to achieve all of this while leaving room for the rest of the meal. The course is about tickling the taste buds rather than filling the stomach.

Choose from the recipes that follow to create your own inviting collage of flavors. Most of these are simple enough to offer easy weeknight options, and several can be made far ahead of time to cut down on the stress and rush before a party or other special occasion. Whichever you choose, they're sure to be a wonderful kickoff to your next culinary celebration.

other ingredients support or reinforce. This is especially true of cold antipasti, which were originally as basic as a saucer of sliced sopressata, a small bowl of cured olives, or a scattering of fresh seasonal fruit.

As uncomplicated and casual as they may be, the artistry of antipasti lies in combin-

# Marinated Button Mushrooms

*Serves 6 to 8*

½ cup olive oil

2 pounds small button mushrooms, cleaned (see page 21)

1½ tablespoons chopped garlic

¾ cup diced Roasted Red Peppers (page 252)

½ cup julienned sun-dried tomatoes

3 tablespoons diced red onion

2 tablespoons chopped fresh basil

2 tablespoons chopped fresh flat-leaf parsley

¼ cup red wine vinegar

1½ teaspoons kosher salt

½ teaspoon cracked black pepper

Button mushrooms don't have the complex flavors that wild varieties such as portobello or chanterelle boast. But that subtlety makes them the perfect canvas for a simple but alluring blend of herbs and other ingredients. The vinegar and red onion in this recipe provide the slightest sharp edge, contrasting the sweetness that comes out when the mushrooms are sautéed. Searing mushrooms in this way also gives them a lovely color that complements the reds and greens in the dish.

*1. Heat the olive oil in a large sauté pan over medium-high heat. Add the mushrooms and sauté for about 3 minutes, just until they start to brown.*

*2. Add the garlic and sauté until the mixture begins to pick up color, 2 to 3 minutes. Remove the mixture from the pan and set aside to cool.*

*3. In a large bowl, combine the remaining ingredients. Add the cooled mushrooms to the bowl and mix well. Refrigerate for at least 2 hours prior to serving.*

## CARMINE'S KITCHEN WISDOM

Cleaning mushrooms is one of the most basic techniques in Italian cooking, but also one of the most essential. Even a tiny bit of dirt can make for a gritty mouthfeel that can ruin the dish. Although some people give their mushrooms a quick rinse, at Carmine's we clean our mushrooms using the tried-and-true classic method: brush any dirt off them with a paper towel or clean kitchen towel (you can also purchase a brush made specifically for this purpose through specialty stores). This is a more painstaking way to clean your fungi, but preferable to washing. Mushrooms that absorb too much water won't sauté properly—the moisture will cause the mushroom to steam from the inside out and make it difficult to achieve a good color and "crusty" seared texture on the outside. You can make the most of your cleaned mushrooms by salting them only after they've cooked. The longer mushrooms cook, the more moisture is extracted; if you salt them in the pan, even more moisture will be pulled out. Reserving the salt to the end ensures that the mushrooms stay plumper.

# Crostini with Cannellini Bean Dip

*Serves 8 to 10*

½ cup olive oil blend (3 parts canola oil to 1 part olive oil)

2 tablespoons minced garlic

¾ cup finely diced red onions

2 tablespoons finely chopped fresh basil

2 tablespoons finely chopped fresh flat-leaf parsley

1 tablespoon finely chopped fresh rosemary

Two 19-ounce cans cannellini beans, 1 can drained

1½ teaspoons kosher salt

¼ teaspoon ground white pepper

¼ cup white truffle oil

1 loaf Italian bread or baguette

Extra-virgin olive oil, for brushing the bread

*Crostini* translates to "little toast," but the bread itself is only a platform for this classic antipasto. You can top crostini with an amazing diversity of spreads, but we create an incredibly creamy white bean dip as a great stage for other rustic, herb-driven flavors. The cannellini is a favorite bean in the Italian kitchen; cheap and widely available, the bean has a smooth texture, and offers a subtle flavor. This recipe makes abundant dip; if you're putting together antipasti for a smaller gathering, refrigerate the extra for use as an anytime dip with fresh vegetables or chips, or even as a sandwich spread.

*1. Heat the oil in a medium saucepan over medium-high heat. Add the garlic and onions and sauté for 1 minute. Add the basil, parsley, and rosemary and cook for 1 minute. Add the beans, salt, and pepper and stir to combine. Reduce the heat to low and cook for about 15 minutes, or until the beans begin to break down.*

*2. Pulse the mixture in a food processor until smooth, but still with some chunks remaining in the mixture. Fold in the truffle oil, taste, and season with additional salt and pepper as desired. Refrigerate at least 1 hour, or until ready to serve.*

*3. Preheat the oven to 350°F.*

*4. Cut the bread diagonally into slices about ½ inch thick. Brush the slices lightly with olive oil and sprinkle with kosher salt and cracked black pepper. Spread them out on a sheet pan and toast until they turn golden brown. Remove from the oven and let cool for about 3 minutes. Smear with a dollop of the bean dip and serve.*

# THE ITALIAN PANTRY: HEAVENLY OLIVE OIL

Cooks have used olive oil for almost as long as there have been cooks. Cultures from the Pharaohs' Egypt to Socrates' Greece have embraced its charms, and have even used it as a moisturizer, lubricant, and furniture polish. But it took the Italians—particularly Southern Italians—to raise the use of this luscious, savory ingredient to a culinary art form.

High levels of monounsaturated fat help olive oil bolster "good" cholesterol, and ensure a lengthy shelf life. An abundance of polyphenols and other antioxidants means that this "liquid gold" can play a role in preventing cardiovascular disease and promoting good general health.

Travel the length and breadth of the Mediterranean and you'll encounter hundreds of olive varieties. The oils sparkle with colors from chartreuse to sunshine gold. That's why one bottle may be as different from the next as two wines from competing vineyards.

## Finding the Best, Avoiding the Rest

As with wine, the label on a bottle of olive oil speaks volumes about what's inside. An estate name is a good sign. More definitive indicators include official designations. IGP is the Italian acronym for "Protected Geographical Indication," meaning that the product in the bottle was grown and manufactured mostly within the stated geographical area. DOP translates to "Protected Designation of Origin" (PDO in the rest of Europe). This is a more precise and demanding designation than IGP, requiring that the product be entirely grown and manufactured—using accepted traditional practices—in the area listed.

You'll also find organization stamps that point to quality. These include trade and regional groups, such as the COOC (the California Olive Oil Council) and IOC (International Olive Council), both of which certify the quality of olive oils labeled with their seals.

These designations take on even more weight in light of the fact that America is the target market for many counterfeit products adulterated with less flavorful oils. This is also why the terms "bottled in," "product of" and similar phrases are not relevant; where the oil (or mix of oils) is bottled doesn't have any bearing on where the olives were grown or even processed. The other most common terms you'll find on olive oil labels include:

**Virgin and Extra-virgin:** No chemicals and minimal heat were used in processing the oil. The result is more flavorful and purer. Extra-virgin oil contains less acid and a more desirable flavor than mere "virgin."

**Pure Olive Oil:** As with the term "Olive Oil," this one indicates that the oil in the bottle is a blend of virgin and refined oils ("pure" basically means that no filler oil, such as safflower or canola, was used in the blend). This is considered a lower-quality olive oil than virgin or extra-virgin.

**Cold-pressed:** These words describe a production process in which the oil never exceeds 80°F. This

*(continued)*

is important because heat is enemy number one, quickly degrading any oil's healthy components and flavor. "First Cold Pressed" means that the oil is from the first pressing of the olives—a difference without a distinction.

**Refined Olive Oil:** Refined virgin olive oil refers to an oil that has been further processed to lower acidity and remove flavor imperfections. The process can involve filtering the oil through both chemical and charcoal filters and subjecting it to heat.

Technically, these terms have no regulated meaning in the United States. Find "U.S" in front of any of these terms, however, and it means the USDA has inspected and verified that the oil meets the claims associated with each term.

A term universally respected is USDA Organic. This means the oil has met rigid production and handling standards, and that no chemicals were used in growing or processing the olives. Producers have to pay for the privilege of certification, so the absence of this seal on a bottle of organic olive oil doesn't necessarily mean that the oil is of lower quality.

As illuminating as labels may be, ultimately, nothing beats a taste test. Your best bet may be trying a few different olive oils bought in the smallest quantity available. Choose your favorites among those to buy in larger amounts.

## Olive Oil in Action

Carmine's chefs are very careful to use olive oil to its best advantage, and home cooks will get the most out of their oil and their culinary creations if they think like a chef. Because of its relatively low "smoke point" (the temperature at which the oil begins to burn off and becomes less effective as a cooking fat), olive oil should never be used for high-temperature (anything over 300°F) cooking processes such as deep-frying. Use a different oil where the oil is solely a base and not a flavoring agent.

When it comes to using olive oil, stocking more than one is a pro strategy. The chefs in Carmine's kitchen keep a rich, strongly flavored, extra-virgin olive oil on hand for cold sauces and other high-profile uses such as vinaigrette or drizzling over Insalata Caprese. We use milder, less expensive virgin oil for sautéing, and combine it in a blend with canola oil (three parts canola oil to one part olive oil).

## Preserving the Goodness

Proper storage is essential to retaining olive oil's flavor and health benefits. The key is to avoid the four villains: heat, light, air, and age. The olive oil we use in Carmine's kitchen is never allowed to get warmer than 70°F (experts recommend an ideal storage temp of around 55°F). We keep large, stainless steel cans of it in a cool, dark corner of the kitchen, pouring out smaller amounts to use in each night's cooking.

Never store olive oil in plastic containers because the oil can leach harmful compounds out of the plastic. Instead, keep it in an opaque, tightly sealed glass or non-reactive metal container. You can refrigerate olive oil, with the exception of extra-virgin. Refrigeration could noticeably undermine the flavor and texture of the oil. In any case, fresher is always better. Check the "best by" date on the container and dispose of any oil approaching the two-year mark.

# Cured Salmon with Lemon Mascarpone

*Serves 8 to 10*

## SALMON

One 2-pound Norwegian salmon fillet, center cut, skin and pin bones removed

2 teaspoons cracked black pepper

$1/2$ pound kosher salt

$1/2$ pound granulated sugar

Stalks and fronds of 2 fennel bulbs

$1/4$ cup bourbon

$1/4$ cup packed dark brown sugar

## LEMON MASCARPONE

$1/4$ pound mascarpone cheese

2 tablespoons fresh lemon juice

1 teaspoon lemon zest

$1/2$ teaspoon chopped fresh flat-leaf parsley

1 loaf Italian bread (optional)

Curing fish originated as a method to preserve a highly perishable foodstuff. But as this recipe proves, it's also a fantastic way to saturate the fish with intriguing and enchanting flavors. In this case, the hearty nature of wild salmon is tempered by a faint hint of licorice from the fennel and the smokiness of bourbon. Combine it with the tantalizingly smooth and creamy texture of mascarpone and an explosion of bright, crisp flavors, and the salmon steals the spotlight when combined with other appetizers.

*1. Dust the salmon all over with the pepper. In a small bowl, combine the salt and sugar and mix well.*

*2. Cover a large work surface with a piece of plastic wrap. Lay half of the fennel tops over an area about the size of the fillet. Spread about half the salt mixture over the tops.*

*3. Lay the fillet on the salt mixture and spread the remaining mixture over the top. Top the fillet with the remaining fennel stalks and fronds and wrap tightly in plastic wrap. Lay the wrapped fillet on a sheet pan. Cover with another sheet pan, and place a few heavy cans or other weights on top, distributing the weight evenly.*

*4. Refrigerate the salmon for 48 hours, flipping it every 12 hours. After 48 hours, remove the salmon from the refrigerator and unwrap it. Gently remove the fennel, and brush off the salt mixture. Towel the fillet dry.*

*5. In a small pot over medium heat, combine the bourbon and brown sugar and stir until the sugar dissolves. Remove from the heat and let cool.*

6. *Lightly brush the top and bottom of the fillet with the bourbon mixture and return it to the refrigerator for at least 2 hours prior to serving.*

7. *In the meantime, in a small bowl, combine all the ingredients for the lemon mascarpone and mix thoroughly with a fork until completely blended.*

8. *The salmon should be cold and firm when you cut it. Use a sharp, thin knife to cut the fillet from left to right on the diagonal, into very thin slices. Serve the slices with the lemon mascarpone on the side or, as we do at Carmine's, on sliced Italian bread.*

# Rolled Beef with Hot Cherry Peppers

*Serves 8 to 10*

2 pounds beef top round

¼ cup plus 2 tablespoons olive
   oil blend (3 parts canola oil to
   1 part olive oil)

1¼ teaspoons kosher salt

½ teaspoon cracked black pepper

1 cup finely diced yellow onion

1 cup seeded and thinly sliced
   hot Italian cherry peppers

1 cup finely diced red bell peppers

1 tablespoon chopped garlic

½ pound fresh mozzarella cheese,
   thinly sliced

½ cup chopped fresh basil

This hearty beef dish is a wonderful counterpoint to other antipasti, but it can also hold its own as a sturdy appetizer in a multicourse meal. The abundance of savory flavors are cut through with a shot of heat courtesy of the Italian cherry peppers. These peppers are an Italian dinner table favorite. Paired with Carmine's own homemade savory aioli, this is definitely in the running for the title "King of Antipasti."

*1. Cut the beef into large, thin uniform slices. Line a sturdy work surface with thick plastic wrap. Lay the beef slices on the surface (one at a time if the space is limited). Cover with thick plastic wrap and pound them out to a thickness between ¼ and ⅛ inch. Season the slices with ¼ cup of the oil, 1 teaspoon of the salt, and ¼ teaspoon of the pepper.*

*2. Preheat a large sauté pan over high heat. Sear each slice of meat on both sides, about 1 minute per side. Set the meat aside to cool.*

*3. Heat the remaining 2 tablespoons oil in a separate large sauté pan over medium-high heat. Add the onion, hot cherry and bell peppers, garlic, and the remaining ¼ teaspoon salt and ¼ teaspoon black pepper. Sauté until the vegetables pick up some color, 3 to 5 minutes. Remove from the heat and set aside to cool.*

*4. Cover a work surface with plastic wrap and lay out the slices of beef. Top each slice with a slice of mozzarella, and then a sprinkling of the basil. Spread the vegetable mixture on top of the cheese and roll up the beef, ensuring the filling stays intact.*

*5. Wrap individual pieces in plastic wrap. Refrigerate overnight. Slice and serve with Herbed Aioli (page 245).*

# Naples-Style Cauliflower with Lemon and Anchovy Vinaigrette

*Serves 4 to 6*

## SALAD

1 head cauliflower, cut into small florets

1 red bell pepper, cored, seeded, and diced

$1/2$ cup finely diced gherkin pickles

$3/4$ cup canned artichoke hearts, quartered

$1/4$ cup cocktail onions

2 tablespoons capers, drained

## DRESSING

$1/2$ cup olive oil

3 tablespoons fresh lemon juice

1 tablespoon aged red wine vinegar

1 tablespoon chopped fresh flat-leaf parsley

8 anchovy fillets, minced

This recipe is actually similar to the classic Neapolitan Christmas salad. The cauliflower serves as a super stage, helping the colors and textures of other vegetables pop out. That makes the salad a visual delight, with red, white, and green echoing the tricolors of the Italian flag. The fresh sweetness is cut through with a piquant dressing that perfectly balances the saltiness of anchovies with citrus acidity. It's the symmetry of all those different elements that makes this salad a success.

*1. Fill a medium pot three-quarters full with salted water. Bring to a boil over high heat. Add the cauliflower and cook until just tender, about 3 minutes; be careful not to overcook. Drain the cauliflower and set it aside to cool.*

*2. In a large mixing bowl, combine all the dressing ingredients and whisk to blend. Add the remaining salad ingredients, and then gently incorporate the cauliflower with a spoon.*

*3. Refrigerate for about 2 days before serving, for best results.*

# Grilled Shrimp with Fennel

*Serves 4 to 6*

## SHRIMP AND MARINADE

12 jumbo shrimp, peeled and deveined

2 tablespoons extra-virgin olive oil

$^1/_2$ teaspoon chopped garlic

1 tablespoon chopped fresh basil

$^1/_4$ teaspoon kosher salt

## SALAD

2 bulbs fennel (about 1$^1/_2$ pounds total), trimmed, cored and thinly sliced

3 navel oranges, peeled and segmented

$^1/_2$ cup pitted and thinly sliced green Cerignola olives

2 tablespoons julienned mint leaves

$^1/_4$ cup fresh orange juice

1 tablespoon fresh lemon juice

$^1/_4$ cup extra-virgin olive oil

1 teaspoon kosher salt

$^1/_4$ teaspoon ground white pepper

This dish is a salute to summer and al fresco dining, because it plays the natural sweetness of grilled shrimp against the sharper, vibrant tones of mixed citrus juices. Grilling brings out the best flavor in shrimp, but it's essential to get it right. The secret is to keep a close eye on your shrimp and remove them as soon as they're cooked. The shrimp is done when it has completely changed color, to pure white and pink. The grill time should be 4 to 6 minutes total; half the cooking time for each side.

*1. In a small bowl, combine the cleaned shrimp and marinade ingredients. Refrigerate for at least 1 hour.*

*2. Preheat a grill or grill pan over medium heat.*

*3. Remove the shrimp from the marinade and discard the marinade. Grill the shrimp for 2 to 3 minutes on each side, or until charred and firm. Remove from the heat and set aside.*

*4. In a large bowl, combine the salad ingredients and toss to mix. Slice the shrimp in half lengthwise and add to the salad. Refrigerate for at least 1 hour prior to serving.*

# Orzo and Fresh Tuna Salad

*Serves 6 to 8*

## SALAD

¹/₂ pound orzo

¹/₂ pound fresh yellowfin tuna loin, sushi grade

¹/₂ cup finely diced celery

¹/₂ cup finely diced red onions

¹/₂ cup finely diced red bell peppers

Lemon wedges, for garnish

## DRESSING

¹/₂ teaspoon dried oregano

³/₄ teaspoon kosher salt

¹/₄ teaspoon cracked black pepper

¹/₄ teaspoon Tabasco sauce

1 tablespoon chopped fresh flat-leaf parsley

1 tablespoon chopped fresh basil

¹/₄ cup fresh lime juice

¹/₂ cup extra-virgin olive oil

¹/₄ teaspoon crushed red pepper flakes

2 tablespoons red wine vinegar

Orzo is the Italian term for "barley," but orzo pasta is actually made from semolina flour and shaped like large grains of rice. Combining the chewiness of pasta with the flavor-grabbing properties of rice, orzo can be the best of both worlds. Tuna is one of the best fish to use raw in a crudo dish (see "Speaking Italian," page 39) such as this because the fish is possibly the least fishy of seafood. To get the most out of what you buy and this recipe, use only superfresh, sashimi-quality tuna from a reputable seafood shop.

1. *Fill a medium saucepan three-quarters full with heavily salted water. Bring to a boil over medium-high heat. Add the orzo and cook to al dente, 8 to 10 minutes, stirring occasionally to prevent the orzo from sticking together. (If the package directions suggest otherwise, follow the directions for the brand of orzo you've purchased.)*

2. *Finely dice the tuna; freezing it for 2 hours prior will make it easier to cut. Refrigerate until thoroughly chilled (if you've frozen the tuna before cutting, you don't need to chill it).*

3. *In a small bowl, whisk together all the dressing ingredients. Add the chilled tuna and refrigerate for 1 hour.*

4. *Remove and fold in the pasta and salad vegetables and refrigerate for 20 minutes prior to serving. Serve on individual salad plates garnished with a lemon wedge.*

# Farro with Wild Mushrooms

*Serves 4 to 6*

1 pound farro

¹/₂ cup olive oil blend (3 parts canola oil to 1 part olive oil)

1¹/₄ cups thinly julienned red onion

4 ounces porcini mushrooms, cleaned, stems trimmed, mushrooms thinly sliced

4 ounces oyster mushrooms, cleaned, cut into uniform, small pieces

4 ounces portobello mushrooms, cleaned, stems and gills removed, caps thinly sliced

4 ounces button mushrooms, cleaned, stems trimmed, mushrooms thinly sliced

1¹/₂ cups chicken stock (or substitute mushroom or vegetable stock)

¹/₂ teaspoon cracked black pepper

¹/₂ cup chopped pimientos

1 tablespoon brine from a jar of sweet cherry peppers

1 tablespoon kosher salt

¹/₄ cup Balsamic Vinaigrette (page 73)

2 tablespoons white truffle oil

This wonderfully adaptable grain—it's actually hulled wheat—has a light nutty flavor, just slightly stronger than brown rice. It also has an appealingly puffy, crunchy texture when cooked, giving it a shape that is ideal for capturing juices, oils, and flavors. In this antipasto, the farro adds substance and light texture to a blend of mushrooms. The combination of different wild mushroom varieties gives the dish a savory symphony of earthy flavors, while the spices lift those flavors, adding a bit of life and zest to what is a memorable grain salad.

*1. Soak the farro in cold water overnight. Drain and set aside.*

*2. Heat the oil in a large sauté pan over medium-high heat. Add the red onions and cook until they are translucent. Add the farro and all of the mushrooms and sauté for about 5 minutes.*

*3. Add the stock, black pepper, pimientos, and pepper brine and cook until the farro is tender (follow the instructions on the package). Remove from the heat and stir in the salt, vinaigrette, and truffle oil. Let cool before serving in a large bowl.*

# Cubanelle Peppers Stuffed with Three Cheeses

*Serves 6 to 8*

1 pound medium cubanelle peppers (6 to 8 peppers)

4 tablespoons extra-virgin olive oil

1/2 teaspoon chopped fresh garlic

2 tablespoons plus 1 teaspoon coarsely chopped fresh basil

4 teaspoons chopped fresh flat-leaf parsley

1/4 teaspoon kosher salt

Pinch of cracked black pepper

4 ounces roasted red peppers

4 ounces fresh mozzarella cheese, finely diced

4 ounces aged provolone cheese, finely diced

4 ounces whole-milk ricotta cheese

2 ounces sweet sopressata

Balsamic vinegar, for drizzling

The only thing better than one classic Italian cheese, is three classic Italian cheeses. That tempting trifecta serves as the delectable heart of this stuffed pepper dish. As if the combination of very different cheeses wasn't enough to put it over the top, we include a medley of fresh herbs along with the hearty goodness of sweet Italian salami. Although bell peppers are commonly used for stuffing, we prefer the nuanced sweetness, thinner flesh, and more interesting shapes of cubanelles. These are green if picked early, but a deep, attractive red when mature.

*1. Preheat the oven to 350°F.*

*2. Rinse the cubanelle peppers and pat dry. Cut off the top of each and remove the seeds through the opening. Lightly coat the peppers with 2 tablespoons of the olive oil and arrange on a sheet pan. Roast for 10 to 12 minutes, turning halfway through cooking. Remove from the oven and set aside to cool.*

*3. In a small bowl, combine the remaining 2 tablespoons olive oil, the garlic, 1 teaspoon of the basil, 1 teaspoon of the parsley, the salt, and pepper. Mix well. Add the roasted red peppers and refrigerate the mixture for at least 1 hour, or for up to 6 hours.*

*4. In a small bowl, combine the cheeses, the remaining 2 tablespoons basil and 3 teaspoons parsley, the red pepper mixture, the sopressata, and the remaining 2 tablespoons olive oil. Blend well.*

5. *Using a small spoon, carefully fill each pepper completely to the top with the filling. Tightly wrap each stuffed pepper individually in plastic wrap and refrigerate for at least 2 to 4 hours.*

6. *When ready to serve, unwrap each pepper and slice into 3 to 4 pieces. Drizzle with balsamic vinegar before serving.*

## ──── SPEAKING ITALIAN ────

Crudo may not strike the ear as a word describing something delectable, but if you're a fan of raw fish, it will be music to your taste buds. It translates to "raw," and describes a category of cold antipasti that is akin to sashimi (although technically speaking, you can also serve *carne crudo*—raw meat dishes like steak tartare or carpaccio). These raw-fish appetizers are among the simplest of antipasti, accented by oils and vinegars, and perhaps a sprinkling of herbs and spices, meant only to bring out the best in a given fish's flavor.

# Roasted Eggplant Dip

*Serves 4 to 6*

2 medium eggplants

1 tablespoon kosher salt

$^1/_2$ teaspoon cracked black pepper

$^1/_2$ cup extra-virgin olive oil

2 tablespoons chopped garlic

$^1/_2$ cup diced roasted red pepper

1 tablespoon drained capers

5 green Cerignola olives, pitted and diced

2 tablespoons chopped fresh basil

1 tablespoon chopped fresh flat-leaf parsley

1 teaspoon chopped fresh oregano

1 tablespoon fresh lemon juice

$^1/_4$ teaspoon Tabasco sauce

2 teaspoons honey

Sometimes simple is best. This easy-to-make and easy-to-eat healthy dip is the ideal supporting player to a large platter of antipasti, especially one that includes Italian flat bread (like the Tomato Focaccia on page 184), or even raw vegetables. It's a wonderful option for any vegetarians in the crowd. When not serving as an antipasto, it's excellent as a good-for-you alternative to sour cream–based or other fat-heavy dips on movie night or game day.

*1. Peel the eggplants and dice them into uniform $^1/_2$-inch pieces. In a medium bowl, combine the eggplant, salt, black pepper, olive oil, and garlic and toss until evenly coated.*

*2. Preheat a large sauté pan over medium heat.*

*3. Sauté the eggplant until tender, 5 to 7 minutes. Remove the mixture from the pan and set aside to cool.*

*4. In a large bowl, combine the remaining ingredients and blend with a wooden spoon. Add the eggplant and mix until smooth, but still a bit chunky. Refrigerate at least 1 hour, until ready to serve.*

# Romano and Black Pepper Bread Sticks

*Serves 8 to 10*

1 teaspoon active dry yeast

1 teaspoon granulated sugar

3½ tablespoons olive oil blend
(3 parts canola oil to 1 part olive oil),
plus more for the pans and brushing

1 tablespoon kosher salt

5 cups bread flour

## TOPPING

1½ cups grated Romano cheese

2 teaspoons cracked black pepper

4 tablespoons olive oil blend (3 parts
canola oil to 1 part olive oil)

Bread sticks are the unsung heroes of the antipasti platter. They can provide the stage for dips of all kinds, offering a bit of contrast to richer antipasti. These bread sticks are heavenly served warmed and aromatic, but they can keep just as well. Store any extra in an airtight container.

*1. In a stand mixer equipped with a dough hook, combine 1½ cups of warm tap water and the yeast. Mix on low until the yeast has fully dissolved. Add the sugar and continue mixing until it dissolves. Add the oil and salt, and mix for 2 minutes. Slowly add the flour while mixing, until the consistency is smooth.*

*2. Transfer the dough to a floured work surface. Divide the dough into two separate and equal balls. Loosely cover with a clean kitchen towel and let rest for 1 hour.*

*3. Preheat the oven to 350°F. Oil two sheet pans.*

*4. In a small bowl, combine the topping ingredients and mix thoroughly.*

*5. Roll out each ball of dough into a rectangle approximately 1/16-inch thick. Lay the rolled dough on a sheet pan. Repeat with the second ball of dough.*

*6. Lightly brush each rectangle of dough with olive oil, and sprinkle with an even coating of the topping. Using a pizza cutter or small knife, cut the dough into 1-inch-wide strips lengthwise.*

*7. Bake for 20 minutes or until golden brown. Remove from the oven and let cool before serving.*

# Hot Appetizers

Sea Scallops Wrapped in
    Pancetta   46

Wild Mushroom Polenta   48

Artichoke Dip with Mushrooms
    and Arugula   49

Pizza Rustica   52

Stuffed Eggplant Rollatini   54

Stromboli with Pepperoni and
    Cheese   56

Chicken Sausage with Broccoli
    Rabe   58

Stuffed Zucchini   59

Classic Arancini with Prosciutto
    and Peas   60

Mozzarella en Carozza   63

Stuffed Mushrooms   64

Calamari Neapolitan Style   65

Scarpariello Chicken Wings   66

Warm dishes provide a completely different and intriguing element to the antipasti platter. Where cold options make wonderful accents to warm-weather dining and meals outside, hot antipasti are especially comforting first courses for cozy indoor meals with friends and family during colder weather. Really, though, these recipes are yet another interesting way to mix up the selection of antipasti you serve, whenever you serve it. The most intriguing antipasti platter will include both warm and cold dishes.

The culinary creations in this chapter provide more than just appealing diversity and appetite-whetting contrast; they also bring stronger, scintillating aromas than cold recipes can provide. The greater variety of cooking processes involved in crafting these recipes expands the possibilities for tickling the nose. Imagine the alluring sizzle and smell of lightly seared seafood like the Sea Scallops Wrapped in Pancetta (page 46), or the tantalizingly rich aroma of melting cheese from Mozzarella en Carozza (page 63). Italian food is the most sensuous of all cuisines, so it only makes sense that an antipasti platter should appeal to all the senses; the visceral olfactory indulgence of sautéed garlic and onions is just another part of a complete culinary picture.

Like their colder counterparts, many of these recipes can be prepared—in all or part—ahead of time to make bringing a full platter together easier and less stressful. You can also save leftover portions, not only for reuse, but for reimagining as well. Extra amounts of many of these can be incorporated into other main course dishes, and we've offered suggestions on how to do just that in the recipes that follow.

A word of caution: Hot antipasti often incorporate richer ingredients, making balance in your antipasti selection even more important. It's wise to keep in mind that you don't want to overwhelm the palate or the stomach. The danger with any of these, as with all the best antipasti, is that the flavors tempt your guests too much and they overindulge to the detriment of the courses that follow. Keep in mind that if you fall in love with one or another of these wonderful recipes, they can all be converted into main courses. Whatever the case, and however you press these into action, *buon appetito*!

# Sea Scallops Wrapped in Pancetta

*Serves 4 to 5*

1 pound (U-10) dry-packed sea
scallops

1 tablespoon extra-virgin olive oil

1/2 teaspoon chopped garlic

1 1/2 teaspoons chopped fresh basil

1 1/2 teaspoons chopped fresh
flat-leaf parsley

1/8 teaspoon dried oregano

1/8 teaspoon cracked black pepper

1/2 pound pancetta, sliced in half
lengthwise, then very thinly sliced
into half circles

One of the most important lessons to learn in all Italian cooking is that maintaining balance is key. Searing brings out the runaway, impossibly rich sweetness of sea scallops; pancetta embraces each scallop and keeps that sweetness in check with its own characteristic meaty saltiness. You won't find a more delectable marriage. It's rare that any of these culinary gems are left on the plate, but if you do wind up with extra, add them to a simple marinara over spaghetti for a spectacular quick weeknight pasta dish.

*1. Remove the side muscles from the scallops (if any are still attached). Rinse and pat the scallops dry. Slice each in half across the face, so that you have two half-moons.*

*2. In a small bowl, combine all of the other ingredients except for the pancetta. Mix well. Add the scallops to this marinade and refrigerate for 20 minutes.*

*3. Preheat the oven to 350°F. Line a sheet pan with parchment paper.*

*4. Lay out the sliced pancetta and place a marinated scallop at the end of each slice. Roll the scallop up in the pancetta, and skewer it with a long wooden toothpick. Arrange the scallops on the sheet pan and bake for 15 to 20 minutes, or until the pancetta is crisp and the scallops are cooked through. Serve hot.*

# CARMINE'S KITCHEN WISDOM

Getting scallops from the water to the market is a tricky business because they are so perishable. Producers have come up with a lot of strategies to help this shellfish make the trip. Some are straightforward and some a bit more dubious. It's reasonable to assume that fresh is better frozen, but this is only true if you live near a coast and the fresh scallops are truly fresh. Older fresh scallops are inferior to fresh frozen scallops. If the fresh scallops offered locally look a little long in the tooth, try to find IQF (individually quick frozen) scallops.

Preservation is another hot issue when it comes to scallops. Carmine's uses only dry-packed scallops. "Wet-packed" scallops are treated with the preservative sodium tripolyphosphate (known as "STP"). The critical compound is "phosphate"—the same additive that makes detergent work. That's why wet-packed scallops often have a soapy flavor, and why dry-packed scallops are preferable. Dry-packed scallops contain less moisture and have a better texture, shrink less during cooking, and are a better value even at a higher price (less liquid means more scallops per pound).

If you absolutely can't find fresh, dry-packed or quality frozen scallops, clean wet-pack scallops thoroughly before cooking with them. Rinse them and then soak in a lightly salted solution of cold water, for about 10 minutes. Rinse again and pat dry—you should have removed all traces of the syrupy, white STP.

Of course, shopping for scallops goes beyond packaging; you'll also need to understand sizing. Scallops, like shrimp, are sold by the number per pound. For instance, "20/30" scallops means 20 to 30 individual scallops per pound. The U-10 scallops we use in our Sea Scallops Wrapped in Pancetta are usually just under 10 to a pound. Larger sea scallops are easier to cook. Smaller bay scallops cook much more quickly and are susceptible to overcooking, which can result in an unappealing rubbery texture.

# Wild Mushroom Polenta

*Serves 6 to 8*

3 tablespoons olive oil blend
(3 parts canola oil to 1 part
olive oil), plus more for the pan

1 tablespoon chopped shallots

2 ounces porcini mushrooms,
cleaned, stems trimmed,
mushrooms thinly sliced

2 ounces oyster mushrooms,
cleaned and diced

2 ounces portobello mushrooms,
cleaned, stems and gills removed,
caps thinly sliced

2 ounces crimini mushrooms,
cleaned, stems trimmed,
mushrooms thinly sliced

6 tablespoons Pinot Grigio

2 1/2 cups chicken stock

1 cup heavy cream

2 tablespoons unsalted butter

1 teaspoon kosher salt

1/4 teaspoon ground white pepper

1 cup cornmeal

3 tablespoons chopped fresh basil

2 tablespoons chopped fresh
flat-leaf parsley

1 cup grated Romano cheese

The beauty of understated polenta lies in its adaptability. Largely neutral on the tongue, polenta works perfectly with sweet or savory flavors. It can also be used as a stage for stronger flavors, or they can be blended right into the polenta as they are in this recipe. The delicate and exceptional flavors of the wild mushrooms used here find their finest expression in the body of the baked polenta. Classic herbs and simple spices round out the dish, but it's the mushrooms that come forward and help make this an invitingly salty but complex bread substitute.

*1. Lightly oil a quarter sheet pan. Heat the oil in a medium saucepan over medium heat. Add the shallots and cook for 2 minutes.*

*2. Increase the heat to high and add all the mushrooms. Cook until the mushrooms are evenly browned. Add the wine and cook until the liquid has reduced by half. Add the chicken stock, cream, butter, salt, and pepper and bring to a boil; reduce to a simmer.*

*3. Add the cornmeal and stir vigorously, until the cornmeal is tender, about 20 minutes. Add the basil, parsley, and cheese, reserving about 2 tablespoons of the cheese for serving, and stir to incorporate. Pour the polenta onto the prepared quarter sheet pan and refrigerate for 2 hours, or until set.*

*4. When ready to serve, preheat the oven to 375°F.*

*5. Cut the polenta into individual, bite-size portions. Arrange on a cookie sheet and sprinkle with the reserved 2 tablespoons cheese. Bake for 10 to 15 minutes, or until lightly browned. Serve immediately.*

# Artichoke Dip with Mushrooms and Arugula

*Serves 6 to 8*

2 tablespoons olive oil

3 tablespoons finely diced red onion

1 tablespoon chopped garlic

2 ounces crimini mushrooms, cleaned and quartered

1 cup drained and quartered artichoke hearts

1/4 cup trimmed and sliced (1-inch strips) arugula

1/4 cup Pinot Grigio

1 cup mayonnaise

1 cup mascarpone cheese

1/2 cup grated Romano cheese

6 ounces whole-milk mozzarella cheese, finely diced

1 teaspoon kosher salt

1/4 teaspoon ground white pepper

2 tablespoons Worcestershire sauce

Artichokes make a purely divine base for a dip, with just enough flavor to add interest, but not so much that it crowds out the other tones. Parmesan is the traditional partner in a dip such as this, but we were in search of a taste and texture explosion when we developed our version, so we included three classic Italian cheeses. The combination gives the dip an alluring texture, amazing depth of flavor, and a richness that simply soars.

*1. Heat the olive oil in a large sauté pan over medium heat. Add the onion and garlic and sauté until lightly browned. Add the mushrooms and cook for 2 to 3 minutes or until they begin to pick up some color.*

*2. Add the artichoke hearts and arugula and cook for 1 minute. Add the wine. When the wine begins to evaporate, cook for 1 minute more. Remove the pan from the heat. Allow the mixture to cool for several minutes before transferring it to a covered glass container. Refrigerate.*

*3. Preheat the oven to 350°F.*

*4. In the bowl of a stand mixer, combine the remaining ingredients and blend. Add the cooled artichoke mix and blend very gently until incorporated.*

*5. Transfer the dip to a 2-quart casserole dish. Bake for 20 to 25 minutes, or until the dip is heated through, the top is browned, and the dip is bubbling. Serve immediately.*

# THE ITALIAN PANTRY

## Discovering *Formaggio Italiano*, the Wonderful Cheeses of Italy

Italians have had a love affair with cheese for almost as long as they've loved cooking (and eating). The charms of what Italians do with sheep and cow's (and occasionally goat's) milk range from delectably sweet to the saltiest of salty flavors. Italian farmers have crafted dozens of varieties, but a select handful of the most delicious Italian cheeses find their way again and again into recipes. These are the most widely available and popular.

Like Italian wines, the best Italian cheeses are labeled with the acronym "DOP" (Denominazione d'origine protetta), meaning "protected designation of origin." This simply means the cheese was produced in the stated region, using internationally accepted methods of manufacture.

Some Italian cheeses are best for cooking, while others are preferred as "table cheese," ideal for eating alone, with a basket of quality crackers or Italian bread. However you choose to eat an Italian cheese, the general rule is to eat the rind on soft cheeses. The rind of semihard or hard varieties is normally trimmed and discarded. Table cheese should be served at room temperature.

**Asiago:** A nutty flavor sets this cow's-milk cheese apart. First made on a plateau of the Veneto foothills in a region of the same name, Asiago is called a semifirm cheese although it becomes firmer with age; extra time adds brio to the flavor, characterized by sweet overtones and a sharp bite. Cut off and discard the rind, and dress a salad with grated Asiago, or grate it over hot pasta.

**Fontina:** Named for Fontinaz, a village in the Val d'Aosta region, the cheese has a smooth texture and subtly nutty and buttery flavor (similar in many respects to Gruyère). More expensive versions are good with crackers or crusty bread, or even with fresh fruit for a simple weekend breakfast. Moderately priced Fontina is ideal for grating over pasta, but the mid-range offerings really come into their own when melted. They will melt to a silky, liquid texture ideal for sauces and hot sandwiches such as panini. Avoid the red wax–encased Danish versions.

**Gorgonzola:** Another cheese named for an Italian village, gorgonzola is produced in two versions by age: Young, it is called dolce (sweet); when older than a year, it's referred to as naturale (aged). Younger versions are creamy and mild, similar to Brie. Older styles are crumbly and sharper, like blue cheese. Both are shot through with veins of blue mold. The cheese at any age is richly spicy. It is a wonderful salad cheese and goes naturally with figs or pears.

**Mascarpone:** Best known as a dessert cheese used in classics like tiramisu, mascarpone is rich, creamy, and sweet—not all that cheeselike. It's closer in texture to cream cheese or crème fraîche. Made with cream rather than milk, the flavor is ironically somewhat milky with just the slightest tang. It is best used where other ingredients deliver stronger flavors.

**Mozzarella:** The truly Italian version is Mozzarella di Bufala, or buffalo's milk mozzarella. This classic has a delicate rich flavor with a slight edge, and a soft, springy texture. Modern versions are more often made with cow's milk (and labeled *fior di latte*), but retain the distinctive egg shape, delicious flavor, and semisoft texture.

**Pecorino:** There are several regional variations of this ancient hard sheep's cheese, the most common being Pecorino Romano. Others are named for the area of production. All are strong, salty, and slightly nutty cheeses becoming harder and more piquant the longer they age. Pecorino is most often used as a meal ender, as part of a light dessert tray of fruits, nuts, and cheese.

**Parmigiano-Reggiano:** Known as the "king of cheeses," Parmigiano-Reggiano is one of the most popular cow's-milk cheeses throughout the world because it's so useful in the kitchen. In Europe, the name Parmesan is trademarked and tightly regulated; elsewhere, it is used for a range of products from heavenly to pedestrian. Look for cheese stamped with the full name, a slightly oily rind, and a straw to amber color. The uncommon, lightly gritty texture makes quality versions of Parmigiano-Reggiano ideal for grating over fresh garden salads, pastas of all kinds, or simple plates of arugula drizzled with olive oil and fresh lemon juice.

**Provolone:** It makes sense to go out of your way to buy a quality, traditional provolone. High-quality provolone is surprisingly flavorful, rich in spice tones, with a touch of tanginess and satisfying saltiness. When melted, its natural flavors blossom and become slightly more pronounced.

**Ricotta:** This crumbly white cheese is extremely mild, incorporated into cooking more for its body than its flavor. Its most common traditional use is as a blank canvas for flavorings in Italian desserts such as cannoli and cheesecake. However, it is also often used as an accent in savory recipes, including pizza.

**Robiola:** This unusual and delectable cheese is a product of the Piedmont region, and can be made from cow, sheep, or goat's milk (and sometimes a combination). It has a wonderful tangy, creamy flavor that, depending on age and the region of production, can be noticeably nutty and sweet, or pleasingly bitter. But even more memorable is the texture, along the lines of Brie. The texture and complex flavor make this an ideal table cheese, traditionally eaten with a tiny drizzle of honey.

**Taleggio:** This is another time-tested Italian cheese. It has a very pronounced, but pleasant cheesy smell, with the distinct flavors of nuts and fruits and a good amount of tanginess. It's a very soft cheese and, at room temperature, it has a creamy texture the consistency of custard.

**Toma:** Little known outside of Italy, Toma is an enchanting cheese, well worth searching for. It is either soft or semihard, and is most often served with a selection of fruit or smeared on a piece of Italian country bread. It is full-flavored with a faint mushroom overtone, creamy and lovely on the tongue. It also melts well.

# Pizza Rustica

*Serves 8 to 10 (one 10½-inch pie)*

### DOUGH

2 cups all-purpose flour

1½ teaspoons kosher salt

2 tablespoons granulated sugar

3 extra-large whole eggs

1 extra-large egg yolk, beaten

### FILLING

3 pounds part-skim ricotta cheese

2 extra-large eggs

1 cup grated Romano cheese

1 cup finely diced prosciutto

⅓ cup chopped fresh flat-leaf parsley

⅓ cup chopped fresh basil

2 cups finely diced, low-moisture mozzarella cheese

1 teaspoon kosher salt

¼ teaspoon ground white pepper

### EGG WASH

1 extra-large egg

2 tablespoons whole milk

If you've ever wondered where the term "pizza pie" comes from, this recipe will clear up any confusion. This dish is an Easter tradition throughout Italy and is a food of fond childhood memories for many an Italian-American. Authentic pizza rustica must have some form of Italian meat in the mix, and although salami is common, we've gone with the slightly more sophisticated choice of prosciutto. Slice the pizza thinly to avoid filling up dinner guests before dinner arrives.

*1. In the bowl of a stand mixer equipped with a dough hook, combine the flour, salt, sugar, and whole eggs and beat on low speed until thoroughly incorporated. Wrap the dough in plastic wrap and refrigerate for at least 1 hour.*

*2. Preheat the oven to 350°F.*

*3. Remove the dough from the refrigerator and divide it into two equal portions. On a cold, floured work surface, roll out one of the portions into a circle about 13 inches in diameter. Lay the dough, centered, in a 10-inch pie pan and smooth to the contours of the pan.*

*4. In a large mixing bowl, combine all the filling ingredients and fold together. Scoop the filling into the pie shell.*

*5. On the same work surface, roll out the other ball of dough as you did with the first. Brush the edge of the dough in the pie pan with the beaten egg yolk, and lay the second circle of dough on top.*

*6. Press the edges of the top and bottom dough circles together to seal the pie edge all the way around. Smooth for a uniform look and trim off any excess dough.*

7. *In a small bowl, whisk together the egg and milk for the egg wash. Brush the top of the pie with the egg wash. Cut a small X in the center of the top to allow steam to escape. Bake for 40 to 45 minutes.*

8. *When the crust is browned, remove the pie from the oven and transfer to a rack to cool for 15 to 20 minutes. Cut into single-serving slices and serve while the pie is still warm.*

# Stuffed Eggplant Rollatini

*Serves 4 to 5*

1 medium eggplant

1½ cups all-purpose flour

6 large eggs

1 cup grated Romano cheese

3 tablespoons chopped fresh flat-leaf parsley

2 cups vegetable oil

2½ cups fresh whole-milk ricotta cheese

1 cup coarsely grated mozzarella cheese

1 tablespoon chopped fresh basil

½ teaspoon kosher salt

⅛ teaspoon freshly ground black pepper

4 cups Carmine's Marinara Sauce (page 251)

This recipe is all about rustic simplicity and how delicious just a few basic ingredients can be. Rollatini is actually a made-up word. The original name of this dish was Involtini di Melanzane, or "little bundles of eggplant," which exactly describes the dish. The secret to our version is that we use only a very light batter on the eggplant, allowing its subtle flavoring to come through. This is a hearty recipe, and you can use smaller eggplants cut thinner if you're looking to use this as one of a larger selection of antipasti.

*1. Cut the ends off the eggplant and discard them. Peel the eggplant and then cut it lengthwise into ¼-inch-thick slices.*

*2. Spread the flour on a large plate. Whisk 5 of the eggs in a shallow bowl, with ½ cup of the Romano cheese and 1 tablespoon of the parsley.*

*3. In a heavy saucepan or a high-sided skillet, heat the vegetable oil over high heat to 325°F.*

*4. Working with a few slices at a time, coat both sides of each slice of eggplant with flour and shake off any excess. Dip the eggplant in the egg mixture to coat both sides and let any excess drip off.*

*5. Using tongs, submerge 3 to 4 eggplant slices in the hot oil. Do not crowd the pan. Fry the eggplant for 1 to 2 minutes on each side or until golden brown. Transfer the eggplant to a plate lined with paper towels, and set aside to cool to room temperature. Repeat with the remaining eggplant slices.*

*6. Preheat the oven to 375°F.*

7. In a large bowl, mix together the ricotta, mozzarella, ¼ cup of the Romano cheese, the remaining egg, remaining 2 tablespoons parsley, and the basil. Add the salt and pepper, taste and adjust the seasonings as necessary.

8. Lay the eggplant slices lengthwise on a work surface. Put about 2 tablespoons of the cheese mixture on each slice, about 2 inches from the end. Roll the end of the slice over the cheese and continue rolling to make the rollatini.

9. Spread 3 cups of marinara sauce on the bottom of a shallow casserole dish large enough to hold the rollatini in one layer. Arrange the rollatini on the sauce and spoon the remaining 1 cup sauce over the bundles. Sprinkle them with the remaining ¼ cup Romano cheese.

10. Place the casserole dish on a sheet pan and transfer it to the oven. Bake the rollatini for 20 to 25 minutes, or until heated through, bubbling and lightly browned. Remove the rollatini from the oven and serve.

# Stromboli with Pepperoni and Cheese

*Serves 8 to 10 (two 16-inch rolls)*

## DOUGH

1 teaspoon active dry yeast

1 teaspoon granulated sugar

1 tablespoon kosher salt

3 1/2 tablespoons olive oil blend
(3 parts canola oil to 1 part olive oil)

1 1/2 pounds bread flour

## HERB OIL

1 1/2 teaspoons chopped garlic

2 tablespoons chopped fresh basil

1 tablespoon chopped fresh flat-leaf parsley

1/2 cup extra-virgin olive oil

1 teaspoon dried oregano

1/2 teaspoon kosher salt

## FILLING

6 ounces aged provolone cheese, very thinly sliced

4 ounces pepperoni, very thinly sliced

12 ounces fresh mozzarella cheese, thinly sliced

2 ounces grated Romano cheese

An Italian-American creation, the stromboli is essentially a rolled-up pizza. In the interest of ease and speed, some cooks simply fold over the dough, creating a savory turnover indistinguishable from a calzone. But we make ours in the more traditional fashion by rolling up the dough to evenly capture all the delicious fillings. Obviously, all those ingredients make for a filling antipasto, which is why the stromboli should be sliced very thinly when joining other taste sensations on an antipasti platter.

*1. In the bowl of a stand mixer equipped with a dough hook, combine 1½ cups warm water with the yeast. Blend on low until the yeast dissolves. Add the sugar, salt, and oil blend, and continue to blend until all the ingredients dissolve. With the mixer running, gradually add the flour and blend until incorporated and a dough ball forms.*

*2. On a cold, floured surface, roll the dough into a smooth ball. Loosely cover the dough with a kitchen towel and set aside in a warm area for 30 minutes.*

*3. Preheat the oven to 350°F. Line a sheet pan with parchment paper.*

*4. On a cold, floured work surface, divide the dough into two separate equal-sized balls. Roll out one of the balls into a rectangle approximately 15 x 10 inches.*

*5. In a small bowl, whisk together all the ingredients for the herb oil until entirely incorporated. Spread about a quarter of the herb oil over the top of the dough. Arrange half of the provolone slices to cover the dough surface. Do the same with half of the pepperoni slices, then half of the mozzarella slices.*

*6. Dust the top with half of the Romano cheese. Roll the dough into a log, starting at one long side, and rolling side to side. Keep the stromboli tight and the filling intact as you roll.*

*7. Smooth the surface of the roll, and place it on the sheet pan. Brush it lightly with about a quarter of the herb oil. Repeat the entire assembly process with the second dough ball.*

*8. Bake both strombolis for 35 to 40 minutes, or until they are heated all of the way through and the outsides are golden brown. Remove from the oven and let cool for at least 10 minutes before slicing and serving.*

# Chicken Sausage with Broccoli Rabe

*Serves 6 to 8*

1¹/₂ pounds broccoli rabe, cut into 2-inch pieces

¹/₂ cup olive oil

¹/₄ cup sliced garlic

1 pound bulk ground chicken sausage

2 tablespoons chopped fresh basil

1 tablespoon chopped fresh flat-leaf parsley

¹/₂ teaspoon crushed red pepper flakes

¹/₂ teaspoon kosher salt

³/₄ cup chicken stock

Broccoli rabe (also called rapini) is a nutrient-packed green with heads that look like broccoli florets. Don't be fooled though; broccoli rabe has a stronger flavor, pleasingly bitter and more interesting than broccoli. That makes it the perfect complement to the spiciness of a good-quality Italian chicken sausage. It can jump-start the tongue for a savory antipasto, or even become a main course when mixed with a shaped pasta such as orecchiette.

*1. Prepare a large bowl with half water and half ice. In a large saucepan over medium-high heat, bring 8 cups of salted water to a boil. Add the broccoli rabe and boil for 2 minutes. Transfer the broccoli rabe to the ice bath. When chilled, drain and pat dry.*

*2. Heat the olive oil in a large sauté pan over medium-high heat. Add the garlic and sauté until browned. Add the sausage and cook until browned. (Break up the sausage when you first put it into the pan, and then don't move it until one side is browned. Flip the sausage and brown the other side.)*

*3. Add the basil, parsley, red pepper flakes, salt, and the blanched broccoli rabe. Add the chicken stock and heat thoroughly, 5 to 7 minutes. Transfer to a serving bowl and serve immediately.*

# Stuffed Zucchini

*Serves 4 to 5 (20 pieces)*

1/2 cup olive oil

1/2 cup finely diced yellow onion

1 1/2 tablespoons chopped garlic

1 red bell pepper, cored, seeded, and finely diced

1 1/2 cups finely diced crimini mushrooms

3 tablespoons chopped fresh basil

2 tablespoons chopped fresh flat-leaf parsley

2 tablespoons chopped sweet Italian cherry peppers

2 tablespoons cherry pepper brine (from the jar of peppers)

1/2 pound Carmine's Bread Crumbs (page 244)

2 tablespoons grated Romano cheese

2 pounds medium zucchini

Here's a vegetarian option for the antipasti platter, and proof positive that "vegetarian" doesn't mean boring. These neat little self-contained savory treats are packed full of fresh garden herbs along with a healthy dose of comforting cheesiness. Bake the zucchini as we do here, and you give it a scrumptious mouthfeel that makes it more than just the holder of filling. It becomes flavored by the other ingredients, creating a bite-size package that just about melts in your mouth.

*1. Heat the olive oil in a large sauté pan over medium-high heat. Add the onions and sauté until translucent. Add the garlic, bell pepper, and mushrooms and sauté until the mixture begins to pick up color.*

*2. Add the basil, parsley, cherry peppers, and brine. Cook for 1 minute more and remove from the heat. Fold in the bread crumbs and grated cheese.*

*3. Transfer to a loosely covered container and refrigerate until chilled, at least 30 minutes.*

*4. Preheat the oven to 350°F. Line a sheet pan with parchment paper.*

*5. Cut the zucchini into 1-inch-thick slices. Sit each slice on end and use a melon baller to scoop out the center halfway down its depth (about 1/2-inch). Fill each zucchini "cup" with about 2 tablespoons of chilled stuffing, being careful not to overfill.*

*6. Arrange the zucchini pieces on the sheet pan. Bake for 15 to 20 minutes, or until the stuffing is golden brown. Serve hot.*

# Classic Arancini with Prosciutto and Peas

*Serves 10 to 12 (about 36 pieces)*

## ARANCINI

6 tablespoons olive oil blend (3 parts canola oil to 1 part olive oil)

1 medium yellow onion, finely diced

1/4 pound prosciutto, finely diced

1 pound Arborio rice

1/2 teaspoon kosher salt

1/8 teaspoon ground white pepper

1 teaspoon saffron

7 cups chicken stock

1/3 cup grated Romano cheese

6 ounces fresh green peas

1/4 cup chopped fresh flat-leaf parsley

1/4 cup finely diced, low-moisture mozzarella cheese

1/2 cup finely diced aged provolone cheese

8 cups canola oil, for frying

## BREADING

1/2 pound all-purpose flour

1 teaspoon kosher salt

1/4 teaspoon freshly ground black pepper

8 extra-large eggs, beaten

1 pound Carmine's Bread Crumbs (page 244)

You've likely come across arancini if you've spent any time in an authentic Northeast pizza parlor, or a true Italian deli anywhere in America. These golden brown rice balls are a staple because they are so flavor-packed and lend themselves to quick meals—and quick antipasti preparation. We stuff our arancini with garden-fresh green peas, a combination of cheeses that offers a little something for every part of your tongue, and a thoughtful selection of spices and herbs that elevates each ball to a taste sensation. We also serve ours the traditional way: hot, with a little Carmine's Marinara Sauce (page 251) on the side.

*1. In a large saucepan over medium heat, combine the oil blend, onions, and prosciutto and sauté until the onion sweats. Add the rice, salt, white pepper, and saffron and stir for 2 minutes.*

*2. Reduce the heat to medium-low. Add the chicken stock ½ cup at a time, stirring continuously until the liquid is mostly absorbed. Continue doing this until all of the stock is used, 20 to 30 minutes.*

*3. Fold in the Romano cheese, peas, and parsley. Transfer the mixture to a sheet pan and refrigerate for about 1 hour.*

*4. In a large bowl, combine the cooled risotto, mozzarella, and provolone, folding in the cheeses. Set aside.*

*5. In a small bowl, mix together the flour, salt, and black pepper for the breading. Place the eggs in a separate bowl, and the bread crumbs in a third bowl. Put the bowls in a row, in the order listed, to create a breading station.*

6. *Roll a 1-ounce ball of the risotto. Dip it in the flour mixture and shake off the excess. Dip it in the egg, allowing any excess to drip off. Then roll the ball in the bread crumbs. Transfer the balls to a sheet pan as you work. Continue until you have breaded all the arancini.*

7. *Heat the canola oil in a large saucepan to 325°F. Working in small batches, fry the arancini just until the outsides become golden brown and the centers are heated through. Serve hot, with a bowl of Carmine's Marinara Sauce (page 251).*

# Mozzarella en Carozza

*Serves 4 to 6*

2 tablespoons extra-virgin olive oil

1 teaspoon chopped fresh basil

2 roasted red peppers, cut into
    4 equal pieces

1/4 teaspoon dried oregano

1/2 teaspoon chopped fresh garlic

8 slices white bread, crusts removed

6 ounces whole-milk mozzarella
    cheese, sliced 1/4-inch thick

4 anchovy fillets

8 whole fresh basil leaves

2 cups canola oil

4 extra-large eggs, beaten

1 tablespoon grated Romano cheese

1 tablespoon chopped fresh flat-leaf
    parsley

Every antipasti platter should include at least one dive into decadence, and this recipe fills the bill in a big way— *en carozza* translates to "in carriage." Our version elevates that basic idea, combining the cheese with roasted red pepper and anchovy for some additional flavor. But make no mistake: the cheese is the master of this creation. Allowed to cool for a few minutes, the individual sandwiches can be quartered into nearly bite-size portions.

*1. In a small bowl, combine the olive oil, chopped basil, roasted peppers, oregano, and garlic. Refrigerate, covered, for at least 1 hour. (You can skip this step if you're using premade Roasted Red Peppers as described on page 252.)*

*2. Top a piece of bread with a slice of mozzarella, an anchovy fillet, 1 piece of roasted red pepper, and 2 basil leaves in that order. Cover with another slice of bread, and pinch the edges to enclose the fillings.*

*3. In a deep sauté pan or high-sided skillet over medium-high heat, heat the canola oil to approximately 325°F.*

*4. In a small bowl, combine the eggs, Romano cheese, and parsley. Dredge each of the sandwiches in the egg wash. Slide them into the hot oil and fry until the undersides are browned (you'll need to hold each sandwich down slightly with a metal spatula while frying, to prevent the slices of bread from separating). Flip each sandwich and brown the other side.*

*5. Transfer the sandwiches to the paper towel–lined plate and allow to cool for several minutes. Serve while still warm, with a side of lemon butter or Carmine's Marinara Sauce (page 251).*

# Stuffed Mushrooms

*Serves 6 to 8 (30 pieces)*

¹/₄ cup olive oil

¹/₂ cup finely diced yellow onion

1 cup finely diced red bell pepper

1¹/₂ tablespoons chopped garlic

1 pound bulk ground chicken sausage

3 tablespoons chopped fresh basil

2 tablespoons chopped fresh flat-leaf parsley

¹/₂ teaspoon crushed red pepper flakes

2 cups chopped broccoli rabe (florets only)

¹/₄ cup dry white wine

¹/₂ cup chicken stock

¹/₄ cup heavy cream

2 cups Carmine's Bread Crumbs (page 244)

¹/₂ cup grated Romano cheese

¹/₂ pound smoked mozzarella cheese, finely diced

30 large white mushrooms, cleaned, stems removed

Turn a mushroom upside down and you quickly discover that it can be an ideal all-in-one container for other flavorful ingredients. Of course, what you fill a stuffed mushroom with is the greater part of the magic. Our filling includes a satisfying bit of chicken sausage with a full slate of spices and herbs, all bound up with our own tasty bread crumb recipe and some purely wonderful cheeses.

*1. Heat the olive oil in a large sauté pan over medium-high heat. Add the onions, bell pepper, and garlic and sauté until the mixture begins to pick up color. Add the sausage and cook until browned.*

*2. Add the basil, parsley, red pepper flakes, and broccoli rabe and cook until the vegetables are tender. Add the white wine and scrape up any bits clinging to the pan. Cook until the liquid has reduced by about half.*

*3. Add the chicken stock and cream, bring to a boil, and fold in the bread crumbs and grated cheese. Remove the pan from the heat and transfer the stuffing to a large bowl. Let cool to room temperature. Fold in the mozzarella and refrigerate.*

*4. Preheat the oven to 350°F. Line a sheet pan with parchment paper.*

*5. Fill each mushroom cap with about 3 tablespoons of the stuffing, being careful not to overfill. Arrange the stuffed mushrooms on the sheet pan.*

*6. Bake for 15 to 20 minutes, or until the mushrooms are thoroughly cooked and the stuffing is golden brown. Serve hot.*

# Calamari Neapolitan Style

*Serves 4 to 6*

3/4 cup olive oil blend (3 parts canola oil to 1 part olive oil)

2 tablespoons chopped fresh garlic

1 pound zucchini, diced

2 pounds fresh calamari, cut into 3/4-inch rings

1/2 pound fresh plum tomatoes, diced

1/4 cup chopped fresh basil

3 dried bay leaves

1/2 cup pine nuts

1/3 cup dried, oil-cured, pitted black olives

1/4 teaspoon crushed red pepper flakes

1 1/2 cups clam juice

The secret to great calamari is to cook it so that it is succulent without becoming rubbery. And that's the secret of this recipe, straight from Naples, the home of the freshest seafood in Italy. The acid of the tomatoes and the moisture from the other juices in the mix help tenderize the squid. The natural flavors of pine nuts and olives moderate the light richness of the seafood and help round out the flavors.

1. Heat the oil in a large saucepan over medium-high heat. Add the garlic and zucchini and sauté for 2 minutes. Add the calamari, tomatoes, basil, and bay leaves and cook for 3 minutes.

2. Add the pine nuts, olives, red pepper flakes, and clam juice. Increase the heat to high, and bring to a boil. Cook for about 15 minutes, or until the liquid has reduced by at least half and the calamari is tender. Transfer to a serving bowl and serve hot.

# Scarpariello Chicken Wings

*Serves 6 to 8 (30 pieces)*

## MARINATED CHICKEN

4 pounds medium chicken wings
(separated at the joint)

1 lemon, halved

2 tablespoons sliced fresh garlic

1 tablespoon chopped fresh
rosemary

1 tablespoon chopped fresh sage

1 tablespoon chopped fresh oregano

1¹/₂ teaspoons kosher salt

¹/₂ teaspoon cracked black pepper

³/₄ cup olive oil blend (3 parts
canola oil to 1 part olive oil)

2 to 3 cups canola oil, for frying

¹/₂ teaspoon cayenne pepper
(optional)

## SAUCE

¹/₄ pound (1 stick), plus 1
tablespoon unsalted butter

1 tablespoon chopped shallots

1 tablespoon chopped fresh rosemary

1 tablespoon chopped fresh oregano

¹/₄ cup white wine

1 cup chicken stock

1 teaspoon Tabasco sauce

¹/₂ teaspoon kosher salt

If you're going to be literal about it, the name translates roughly to "shoemaker-style," but let's not be literal. There's nothing "cobbled" together about this dish that features deeply marinated chicken wings (a spin on a dish traditionally made with chicken pieces with the bone in) full of flavor and dressed in a sauce with just the right amount of fire to keep the dish interesting.

*1. Rinse the chicken under cold water. In a medium bowl, mix all of the marinade ingredients except for the chicken and frying oil. Add the chicken and toss to coat. Cover and refrigerate for at least 48 hours, turning the chicken pieces every few hours.*

*2. In a 3-quart or larger pot over medium-high heat, heat the canola oil to 350°F. Line a plate with paper towels.*

*3. Remove the wings from the marinade and clean off any herbs and garlic. Pat them dry with paper towels. Working in batches to avoid overcrowding, pan fry the wings until they begin to brown on the undersides, then turn them. When browned all over and thoroughly cooked through, 4 to 5 minutes per side, transfer them to the paper towel–lined plate. For an added kick to the dish, toss the wings in ¹/₂ teaspoon of cayenne pepper right after they are fried.*

*4. For the sauce: In a large sauté pan over medium-high heat, melt the 1 tablespoon of butter. Add the shallots and sauté until translucent. Add the rosemary and oregano and sauté for 20 seconds more. Add the white wine and cook until the liquid has reduced by half.*

½ teaspoon crushed red
  pepper flakes

4 cloves Roasted Garlic (page 242)

2 tablespoons fresh lemon juice

**GARNISH**

½ bulb fennel, julienned

1 cup Gorgonzola Dressing (page 74)

*5. Add the chicken stock, Tabasco, salt, red pepper flakes, and roasted garlic. Cook until the liquid has again reduced by half.*

*6. Reduce to a simmer and whisk in the remaining ¼ pound butter. Add the lemon juice. Toss the wings in the sauce for 5 seconds. Spread the wings on a serving platter, covered with the sauce. Serve with the fennel and Gorgonzola Dressing on the side.*

# Salads

Italians approach salads with the same gusto they bring to all the other courses they cook, creating recipes that are alive with bold flavors and interesting textures. Italian salads—like most of the country's dishes—are regional, based largely on the prize edibles from the specific area. For example, the classic Insalata di Carciofi exploits the artichokes of Emilia-Romagna in the north, while Insalata di Mare makes wonderful use of the bountiful seafood caught off the shores of Sicily. Whenever greens are used, they must be washed thoroughly. Something like mixed mesclun greens can be simply rinsed and dried in a salad spinner. Heartier greens may call for a soaking to remove any possible traces of grit.

The focus on freshness extends to the salad dressings. Dressings are where salads often go wrong and, at Carmine's, we would never think of buying premade dressings in bulk. We make our own from scratch (and give you those precious formulas on pages 73 to 74). That's the only way to ensure sunny, vibrant flavors with perfectly balanced spices.

The salad recipes that follow are much more than just tongue-pleasing mid-menu courses. Using the freshest ingredients with minimal processing has other advantages; these are nutrient- and fiber-packed dishes. Each one is a healthy meal and can easily stand in as a light main course.

# Carmine's House Salad Mix

*Yields 4 quarts*

¹/₂ head iceberg lettuce

¹/₂ head escarole

1 small bunch arugula

We use this simple blend as the base for many of our salads, including several in this chapter. Just the same, you can whip this up as a quick, no-worries salad any day of the week. It's a basic mix that includes a little pleasing bitterness and some peppery notes courtesy of the arugula.

*1. Core and coarsely chop the iceberg and escarole into roughly 2-inch pieces. Trim the ends of the arugula (if the leaves are large, cut them into halves and quarters). Wash all the greens in a deep container of cold water, rinse, and spin dry.*

*2. Refrigerate, and toss the salad just prior to serving.*

Salad dressings are the taste signature of any restaurant, and we like ours to be full of sharp, brilliant flavors that bring out the best in any salad's ingredients. Each of these recipes that follow makes a significant amount of dressing; use them as bread dips, or piquant coatings for steamed vegetable. They will all keep, refrigerated, for several weeks.

## Balsamic Vinaigrette

Yields 6½ cups

3 tablespoons chopped shallots

6 tablespoons Dijon mustard

1½ cups aged balsamic vinegar

¼ cup granulated sugar

3 tablespoons fresh lime juice

4 cups olive oil blend (3 parts canola oil to 1 part olive oil)

⅓ cup chopped fresh basil

1¾ teaspoons kosher salt

¾ teaspoon cracked black pepper

In a medium bowl, whisk together the shallots and mustard. Mix in the vinegar, sugar, and lime juice. Gradually add the oil in a slow, steady stream while whisking continuously until all the oil is incorporated. Add the basil, salt, and pepper, and refrigerate until ready to use.

## Creamy Italian Dressing

Yields 2 cups

1 teaspoon chopped shallots

4 tablespoons grated Ricotta Salata cheese

1 egg yolk

⅓ cup white vinegar

1½ tablespoons fresh lemon juice

1½ cups olive oil blend (3 parts canola oil to 1 part olive oil)

1½ teaspoons chopped fresh basil

¼ teaspoon kosher salt

⅛ teaspoon freshly ground black pepper

⅛ teaspoon dried oregano

In a medium bowl, combine the shallots, cheese, egg yolk, vinegar, and lemon juice. Using a hand blender, mix the ingredients. Gradually add the oil in a small steady stream while blending, until all of the oil is incorporated. Mix in the basil, salt, pepper, and oregano. Refrigerate until ready to use.

## Lemon-Basil Vinaigrette

Yields 2 cups

1½ cups olive oil blend (3 parts canola oil to 1 part olive oil)

½ cup fresh lemon juice

4 teaspoons aged red wine vinegar

1 teaspoon chopped shallots

1 teaspoon kosher salt

⅛ teaspoon ground white pepper

¼ cup chopped fresh basil

In a medium bowl, combine all the ingredients. Let sit for 20 minutes before using. Refrigerate in a cruet between uses, and shake just prior to serving.

*(continued)*

## Carmine's Vinaigrette

Yields 2 cups

1½ cups olive oil blend (3 parts canola
    oil to 1 part olive oil)
½ cup aged red wine vinegar
1 teaspoon dried oregano
1 teaspoon kosher salt
¼ teaspoon freshly ground black pepper
1 pasteurized egg yolk

Combine all the ingredients in the bowl of a food processor and blend just until incorporated. Use the dressing right away, or store it in a covered container in the refrigerator for up to 10 days. Whisk before using

## Gorgonzola Dressing

Yields 3 cups

2 cups Hellmann's Mayonnaise
1 cup crumbled Gorgonzola cheese
¼ cup white vinegar
½ teaspoon kosher salt
½ teaspoon cracked black pepper
½ teaspoon Worcestershire sauce
¼ teaspoon dried oregano

In a medium bowl, combine all the ingredients and mix thoroughly, breaking up any large chunks of cheese. Refrigerate for at least 4 hours prior to serving. This also makes a delicious dip!

# Tuscan Bean Salad

*Serves 4 to 6*

1 pound dried cannellini beans

¹/₂ pound pancetta, finely diced

1 cup thinly sliced celery

1 small red onion, halved and thinly sliced

¹/₄ cup finely chopped fresh basil

¹/₄ cup finely chopped fresh flat-leaf parsley

1 cup finely diced sun-dried tomatoes

1 cup extra-virgin olive oil

¹/₂ cup red wine vinegar

³/₄ teaspoon kosher salt

¹/₈ teaspoon cracked black pepper

Among Italians, Tuscans are known as *mangiafagioli,* or "bean eaters," because they love their beans, cannellini first and foremost. This creation surrounds that treasured, creamy white bean with a host of other simple, sturdy ingredients. The bean is justly popular for its smooth, elegant texture and understated nuttiness, making it the ideal canvas for the salty essence of crisped pancetta and hearty richness of sun-dried tomatoes.

*1. Soak the beans overnight. Rinse them and place in a medium pot and cover with fresh cold water. Bring to a boil over medium-high heat, then reduce the heat to a simmer and cook for 30 to 40 minutes until the beans are tender but not broken. Drain and transfer the beans to a bowl to cool.*

*2. In a medium sauté pan over medium heat, cook the pancetta until crispy and the fat has rendered. Transfer to a paper towel–lined plate to dry.*

*3. In a large bowl, combine the beans, pancetta and all the remaining ingredients, gently folding them together. Taste and add salt and pepper as desired. Refrigerate until well chilled. Serve cold.*

# Mesclun Greens with Grilled Vegetables

*Serves 6 to 8*

**MARINATED VEGETABLES**

$^1/_2$ pound zucchini, cut into
small wedges

1 medium carrot, halved lengthwise
and cut into 2-inch pieces

1 red bell pepper, quartered, seeded,
and cut into 2-inch pieces

$^3/_4$ cup extra-virgin olive oil

1 tablespoon chopped fresh basil

1 tablespoon chopped fresh oregano

1 tablespoon chopped fresh rosemary

1 tablespoon chopped fresh flat-leaf
parsley

$^3/_4$ teaspoon kosher salt

$^1/_8$ teaspoon cracked black pepper

1 tablespoon garlic

**SALAD**

$^1/_2$ pound mesclun mix

$^1/_4$ pound grape tomatoes

1 small head radicchio, halved and
thinly sliced

$^1/_4$ pound red onion, julienned

2 ounces black Taggiasca olives
(about 12 olives)

$^1/_8$ teaspoon kosher salt

Pinch of cracked black pepper

$^1/_2$ cup Balsamic Vinaigrette (page 73)

3 ounces crumbled goat cheese

There is no better way to taste summer than to build a salad around grilled vegetables. But as good as grilled vegetables certainly are, we weren't satisfied to stop there. This healthy, stomach-pleasing salad sits atop a bed of greens and special lettuces that just add to the attraction, offering a wealth of texture and turning the salad into a fireworks display on the plate. Olives, onions, and our own balsamic dressing round out a full-bodied salad that is a wonderful introduction to a meat or rich pasta main course.

*1. In a medium bowl, combine all the marinated vegetable ingredients and toss to coat. Refrigerate for 1 hour.*

*2. Preheat the grill or a grill pan over medium-high heat.*

*3. Grill the marinated vegetables for 10 to 15 minutes, or until marked with sear lines and tender. Turn the vegetables often to cook evenly. Set aside to let cool.*

*4. When ready to serve, toss all the salad ingredients except for the goat cheese in a large bowl. Serve on a platter and top with the grilled vegetables and the goat cheese.*

## CARMINE'S KITCHEN WISDOM

Matching wines to a salad involves considering both the salad, and the dressing used. Some ingredients, like radicchio and endive, are more about texture than overarching flavor. More complex ingredients call for balance: balsamic is sweet and a little tart, while citrus, white- and red-wine vinaigrettes are going to present strong acidity. White wines with a fruit-forward flavor and relatively high acidity will marry well with acidic ingredients and dressings. Try a nice Gavi or Pinot Grigio with a higher acidity. Balsamic vinaigrettes do well paired with a rosé, and fruitier whites like Chenin Blanc. Vegetable and bean salads are often best served with leaner, "green" wines, such as a good Soave.

# Asparagus and Fava Bean Salad with Blue Crab

*Serves 6 to 8*

3 pounds fava beans (about 1 pound cleaned)

¹/₄ cup extra-virgin olive oil

¹/₄ pound prosciutto, slivered

¹/₂ cup finely diced yellow onion

2 ounces sun-dried tomatoes, julienned

1 pound fresh asparagus, cut diagonally into ¹/₂-inch pieces

¹/₂ teaspoon kosher salt

¹/₄ teaspoon cracked black pepper

2 tablespoons chopped fresh basil

2 tablespoons chopped fresh flat-leaf parsley

¹/₂ cup Lemon-Basil Vinaigrette (page 73)

¹/₂ pound lump blue crabmeat

A surefire way of creating an incredibly interesting salad is to combine unusual elements and flavors that you wouldn't normally think of together, like the fava beans and crabmeat in this spectacular salad. Cleaning the fava beans is a family tradition in many Italian homes, and it's a fun way to get kids involved in the kitchen. We always use asparagus with stems on the thicker side because they bring a lot more textural interest to the salad.

*1. Clean the fava beans by breaking off the tip where the pod was attached to the plant, and use it to pull the stringlike piece that runs along the seam of the pod. Pull out the beans.*

*2. Fill a small pot with salted water and bring to a boil over medium-high heat. Fill a large bowl with ice and water. Place the beans in the pot, cook for 30 seconds, and transfer to the ice bath. When the beans are cool, drain and peel off the thin outer membrane. Set the peeled beans aside.*

*3. Heat the olive oil in a large sauté pan over medium-high heat. Once hot, add the prosciutto and sauté it until it begins to brown. Add the onion and sauté for 1 to 2 minutes, or until the onions start to become translucent. Add the fava beans, sun-dried tomatoes, asparagus, salt, and pepper and sauté for 3 to 4 minutes, or until the mixture becomes tender. Set aside to cool.*

*4. In a large bowl, combine the cooled beans and vegetables, the basil, parsley, vinaigrette, and crabmeat. Fold together and refrigerate for at least 1 hour. Serve cold.*

# THE ITALIAN PANTRY: TANTALIZING BALSAMIC

Balsamic vinegar has been an incredibly versatile Italian kitchen staple for centuries. High-quality balsamic balances a natural tang with complex raisin, fig, and caramel flavors, and a subtle sweetness. This is because balsamic is made from grape pressings left over from the winemaking process. The grape remnants are not fermented, but are cooked, boiled down to an inky liquid that is then aged in oak with a vinegar "mother." Over time, the liquid is moved from one cask to another, each made of different wood. Those woods impart a variety of flavors to the final product. During the aging process, water evaporates out of the balsamic, so that the vinegar becomes progressively thicker and more intense. The final product is always aged at least 12 years, giving it an alluring syrupy body, with a deep, rich aroma and a complexity that rivals wine.

Not all balsamic is made in this time-honored fashion. Industrialized processes allow manufacturers to make a much less attractive product in hours rather than years. The question is how to tell the difference.

The price tag will be your first clue. Balsamic produced in the traditional fashion will be expensive. Another giveaway is the label. Traditionally, balsamic is made in two regions of Italy: Reggio Emilia and Modena. Balsamic from either region is labeled Aceto Balsamico Tradizionale (di Modena or di Reggio Emilia). Both are designated (and often marked on the label) by the Italian DOP (Denominazione di origine protetta) and the European Union's POD (Protected Designation of Origin). A lesser version of the Modena product is called Aceto Balsamico di Modena.

These are the only true, traditional artisan balsamic vinegars.

A greater number of balsamic vinegars on the American retail shelf are either industrially produced, commercial-grade products, or *Condimento*—a blend of traditional and commercial. That doesn't mean they don't have a place in the kitchen.

A really fine traditional balsamic is equivalent to a high-quality wine; it is usually drizzled directly on fruit and cheese, or vegetables, or used as a dipping sauce for high-quality bread. But much of the magic is lost when the balsamic vinegar is blended with several other strongly flavored ingredients into a salad dressing, or exposed to heat when cooked into a sauce. That's when a less expensive version is fine.

As with olive oils, you'd be wise to work with two different balsamic vinegars in your kitchen. Use a simpler, lower-cost version for sauces, general cooking, and dressings. Keep a more expensive, smaller bottle of aged traditional balsamic on hand for special occasions, such as simple desserts of strawberries and aged Italian cheeses drizzled with balsamic.

# Arugula Salad with Gorgonzola

*Serves 6 to 8*

**MARINATED VEGETABLES**

$1/2$ pound eggplant, cut into
  small wedges

$1/2$ pound button mushrooms, cleaned

1 red bell pepper, quartered,
  seeded, and cut into 2-inch pieces

$3/4$ cup extra-virgin olive oil

1 tablespoon chopped fresh basil

1 tablespoon chopped fresh oregano

1 teaspoon chopped fresh rosemary

1 tablespoon chopped fresh flat-leaf
  parsley

$3/4$ teaspoon kosher salt

$1/8$ teaspoon cracked black pepper

1 tablespoon chopped garlic

**SALAD**

3 ounces crumbled gorgonzola cheese

$1/2$ pound arugula, cleaned

$1/2$ cup julienned red onion

1 head endive, cut into 1-inch pieces

$1/8$ teaspoon kosher salt

Pinch of cracked black pepper

$1/2$ cup Carmine's Vinaigrette
  (page 74)

Peppery arugula provides the enticing foundation for this busy preparation; marinated eggplant and mushrooms offer more exotic flavors and textures. Go the extra mile and spend a bit more for older, high-quality gorgonzola. The bite of an aged version will ensure that the flavor of the cheese is not overwhelmed by the other piquant notes in this filling and scrumptious salad.

*1. In a small bowl, combine the ingredients for the marinated vegetables and toss to coat. Set aside for 1 hour.*

*2. Preheat the oven to 400°F.*

*3. Spread the marinated vegetables out on a sheet pan and roast for 10 to 15 minutes, or until nicely browned. Remove and let cool.*

*4. When ready to serve, combine half the gorgonzola and all the salad ingredients in a large bowl and toss. Serve on a large platter, topped with the roasted vegetables and the rest of the cheese.*

# Spinach and Bocconcini Salad

*Serves 6 to 8*

## BOCCONCINI

$1/2$ pound fresh bocconcini, each piece halved

3 tablespoons extra-virgin olive oil

$1/4$ teaspoon kosher salt

Pinch of cracked black pepper

2 teaspoons chopped fresh basil

$1/2$ teaspoon minced garlic

1 tablespoon chopped fresh flat-leaf parsley

2 tablespoons finely diced Roasted Red Peppers (page 252)

## SALAD

4 ounces sun-dried tomatoes, julienned

$1/4$ teaspoon kosher salt

$1/8$ teaspoon cracked black pepper

2 tablespoons extra-virgin olive oil

6 ounces pancetta, finely diced

$1/2$ pound baby spinach, rinsed

$1/2$ cup julienned red onions

$1/2$ cup Carmine's Vinaigrette (page 74)

A rich and creamy cheese can be just the thing for a meal-starting salad, especially when it's supported by some fresh greens and herbs. Bocconcini is a salad-size variety of mozzarella—individual balls a little bigger than robin's eggs. The mild, semisoft cheese almost seems to grab hold of the spices and herbs in this salad, amplifying their effect. Sun-dried tomatoes and pancetta add salty, dense flavors that paint a vivid picture on the plate and in the mouth. This is one of the more impressive-looking salads you're likely to make, and it is ideal for large, special-occasion meals.

*1. In a small bowl, combine all the ingredients for the bocconcini and toss together. Refrigerate for at least 2 hours.*

*2. In a separate small bowl, combine the sun-dried tomatoes, a pinch each of the salt and black pepper, and the olive oil.*

*3. Preheat a medium sauté pan over medium-high heat. Add the pancetta and cook until crispy. Transfer to a paper towel–lined plate.*

*4. When ready to serve, combine the spinach, onions, and dressing in a large bowl and toss to coat. Spread out on a large platter and top with the pancetta and the marinated sun-dried tomatoes. Arrange the bocconcini nestled in and around the greens.*

# Endive, Arugula, and Radicchio with Romano Cheese

*Serves 6 to 8*

1/4 pound arugula, cleaned and cut into 2-inch strips

2 heads endive, trimmed and cut into 1-inch pieces

1/2 pound radicchio, cut into 2-inch pieces

1 red bell pepper, cored, seeded, and julienned

5 ounces crimini mushrooms, cleaned and sliced

1 small carrot, julienned

1/8 teaspoon kosher salt

Pinch of cracked black pepper

1/2 cup Lemon-Basil Vinaigrette (page 73)

3 ounces shaved Romano cheese

2 ounces black Gaeta olives

2 fresh plum tomatoes, quartered

The flavor combinations in this lovely salad make it one of the liveliest you can put on the table, but it's also one of the easiest to whip up. The multicolored dish includes shades of pleasing bitterness that make each bite jump a little bit on the tongue. There's also plenty of crunch that keeps each mouthful bursting with just-picked freshness. It can also hold its own as a superhealthy lunch or dinner that can be on the table in minutes.

*1. In a large bowl, combine all the ingredients except for the olives and tomatoes, and reserve half of the shaved cheese. Toss to thoroughly mix.*

*2. Spread the salad on the large serving platter and top with the remaining half shaved cheese and the olives. Arrange the tomatoes around the edge of the platter and serve.*

# Mixed Olive Salad

*Serves 6 to 8*

½ pound green Cerignola olives

½ pound oil-cured black Gaeta olives

½ pound green Castelvetrano olives

½ pound black Taggiasca olives

8 ounces Roasted Red Peppers (page 252), julienned (about ¾ cup)

Zest and juice of 2 lemons

Zest of 2 oranges

2 teaspoons chopped fresh rosemary

⅔ cup extra-virgin olive oil

¼ cup finely diced red onion

2 tablespoons crushed garlic

2 tablespoons chopped fresh basil

1 tablespoon chopped fresh flat-leaf parsley

1 teaspoon chopped fresh oregano

The olive groves of Italy yield a head-spinning diversity. We created this salad to showcase four standouts among the harvest, with characters ranging from the sweet, fruity, and mild flavor of the small dark Taggiasca, to the slightly tart and edgier taste of the large green Castelvetrano. Most of the prep time will involve hunting down the olives, which can usually be found in a specialty grocer or a high-end supermarket.

*In a medium bowl, combine all of the ingredients and toss to mix. Cover and refrigerate for 24 hours. Serve on a large platter.*

# Hearts of Romaine with Prosciutto and Ricotta Salata

*Serves 6 to 8*

4 cubanelle peppers, cored and seeded

2 tablespoons extra-virgin olive oil

1½ pounds romaine hearts, halved lengthwise

2 ounces prosciutto, julienned

¾ cup julienned red onion

¾ cup Creamy Italian Dressing (page 73)

2 ounces ricotta salata cheese, grated

1½ ounces black Gaeta olives (about 12 olives)

3 ounces grape tomatoes

Hearts of romaine are an ideal stage on which to showcase other fresh, succulent flavors. The fresh flavor goes with just about any other vegetable, herb, or spice—not to mention the delicate, salty essence of wonderful prosciutto. But it's really the ricotta salata that deserves top billing in this mouthwatering plate filler. This traditional Italian cheese is actually pressed and dried ricotta. The process gives it a slight bit of saltiness, and the faintest hint of milk and nuts.

*1. In a large bowl, combine all the ingredients except for the olives and tomatoes, and reserve half of the grated cheese. Toss to thoroughly mix.*

*2. Spread the salad on the large serving platter. Scatter the tomatoes on top with the remaining half of the grated cheese and the olives.*

# Seafood Salad

*Serves 6 to 8*

1 cup clam juice

12 Littleneck clams, shells rinsed

24 PEI mussels (subsitute a local variety if PEI are not available), shells rinsed

1/2 pound fresh calamari, cut into 3/4-inch rings

1/2 pound precooked scungilli (optional)

1/2 pound jumbo shrimp, peeled and deveined

1/2 pound (U-10) sea scallops

1 cup extra-virgin olive oil

2 tablespoons chopped fresh basil,

2 tablespoons chopped fresh flat-leaf parsley

1 tablespoon, plus 1 teaspoon chopped garlic

1/4 pound red bell peppers, cored, seeded, and finely diced

1/4 pound green bell pepper, cored, seeded, and finely diced

3/4 cup finely diced celery

1/2 cup finely diced yellow onion

1/2 teaspoon dried oregano

1/4 cup fresh lemon juice

1/4 cup aged red wine vinegar

At Carmine's, we believe that if you're going to go to the effort of making a seafood salad, all the frutti di mare should be represented. That's why we include four different types of rich, sweet shellfish, and two different types of squid. We've cut the rich nature of this dish with some basic produce, which also add a bit of crunch to what are otherwise semisoft, melt-in-your mouth textures. The acids in this blend make it an ideal partner to a lovely glass of Falanghina or Vermentino.

1. *In a medium sauté pan over high heat, bring the clam juice to a boil. Add the clams and cover. As the clams open, remove and set aside. Continue cooking until all the clams have opened; discard any that do not open. Repeat with the mussels.*

2. *Add the calamari to the hot liquid and poach for 1 minute. Add the scungilli and cook for 1 minute more. Remove the seafood and set aside.*

3. *Continue to cook the liquid, uncovered, until it has reduced by two-thirds. Transfer to a bowl and let it cool to room temperature. Cover and refrigerate. Remove the clams and mussels from their shells. Combine with the cooked calamari and scungilli in a covered container and refrigerate.*

4. *In a small bowl, combine the shrimp, scallops, 1/2 cup of the olive oil, 2 teaspoons of the basil, 1 tablespoon of the parsley, 1 tablespoon of the garlic, and a pinch of salt and black pepper. Cover and refrigerate for 1 hour.*

1 teaspoon kosher salt

¼ teaspoon cracked black pepper

½ teaspoon chopped fresh oregano

¼ teaspoon crushed red pepper flakes

12 ounces Carmine's House Salad Mix
  (about 8 cups—page 72)

¼ pint grape tomatoes

*5. Spread the marinated shrimp and scallops on a sheet pan and broil on high (or grill if possible) for 2 to 4 minutes, or until cooked. Transfer to a bowl. Refrigerate covered, until chilled.*

*6. In a large bowl, combine all the remaining ingredients, except for the salad greens and tomatoes, and mix well. Add 2 tablespoons of the reduced seafood cooking liquid to the mixture.*

*7. Add all of the chilled seafood, fold together, and let the salad sit for 15 minutes. Taste and add additional salt and black pepper as desired.*

*8. Spread the greens on a large serving platter. Spoon the seafood mixture over the greens. Garnish with the tomatoes around the edges and serve.*

# Pasta

It is simply impossible to imagine an Italian kitchen without pasta. Where would we be without basic spaghetti as a stage for Carmine's signature meatballs? What would all those Italian grandmothers have done for Sunday Dinner without vermicelli to showcase their delectable, slowly simmered meat sauce, or the broad noodles that held a treasured family recipe for lasagna together? Thankfully, we don't have to ponder such things, because Italians long ago ensured that the world would enjoy an abundance of wonderful pasta.

The amazing diversity of this kitchen staple—there are literally hundreds of types—ensures an equally amazing variety of delicious recipes. In reality, the magic isn't in the multitude so much as in the ability of all pastas to grab and hold flavors like no other cooking ingredient. It is perhaps the perfect carrier for sauces both light and heavy, and the ultimate messenger of culinary love letters to the taste buds. Although every culture around the globe has its own style of noodle, it took the Italians to perfect the ideal—a simple, all-occasion standard that elevates

everything it touches and leaves no stomach or appetite wanting.

Like so much else in Italian cooking, there is both a northern and a southern face to this cucina regular. Northerners have traditionally used egg-based pastas made fresh and known as *pasta fresca*. The more down-to-earth Southern and Central Italians historically enjoyed dried pastas (*pasta secca*) made with flour and water, and well suited to long-term storage. In either case, the love of what was traditionally and generically called macaroni in the Old Country and New, runs incredibly deep.

For every pasta there is a wine. It's about the flavors in the sauce. Match tomato-based sauces with fruity wines that have ample acidity and low to medium tannin. You might try a Barbera, the rustic Montepulciano, the Sicilian Nero d'Avola, or Sangiovese-based wines like Chianti. Richer cream-based sauces call for a sturdy white, something along the lines of a Chardonnay.

With all that in mind, the recipes that follow represent some of the most popular pasta dishes we serve. (You'll find general pasta cooking instructions on page 99, rather than repeated in each recipe.) There is great history behind many of these; they have become classic as a consequence of uniquely engaging flavor blends, and the ways in which the particular pasta used brings out the best in the dish. Fortunately, you don't need a restaurant to make the most of this delicious and filling staple. Just set a pot of salted water boiling and prepare to enjoy the glorious wonders of sturdy, simple pasta.

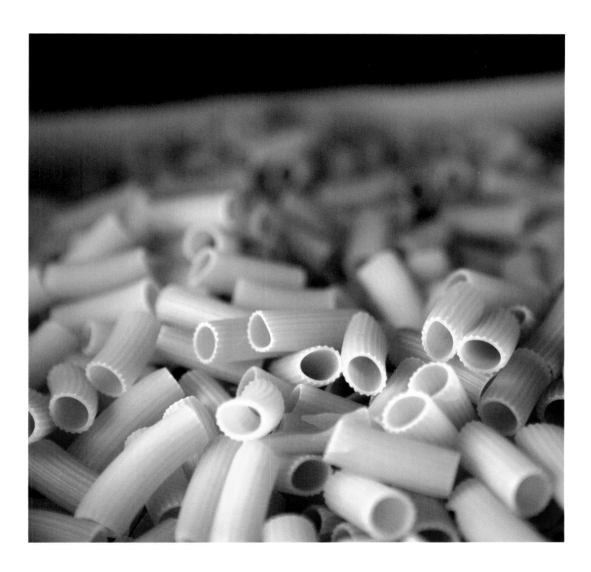

# Orecchiette with Sausage and Broccoli Rabe

*Serves 4 to 6*

¾ cup olive oil

7 ounces Italian chicken sausage

½ cup sliced garlic

½ pound broccoli rabe, trimmed and cut into 2-inch pieces

3 cloves Roasted Garlic (page 242)

¼ cup sun-dried tomatoes, julienned

2 tablespoons chopped fresh basil

1 tablespoon chopped fresh flat-leaf parsley

2 cups chicken stock

½ teaspoon kosher salt

⅛ teaspoon cracked black pepper

12 ounces orecchiette, cooked al dente

¾ cup grated Romano cheese

2 tablespoons Toasted Bread Crumbs (page 246)

Orecchiette translates to "little ears," describing the shape of this distinctive pasta. That shape is important because it is ideal for trapping flavorful juices and bits of spices and herbs, making every bite a tiny celebration. The pasta itself moderates the pleasant bitterness of the broccoli rabe, allowing for the full-bodied flavor of the greens to shine through. The broccoli rabe, for its part, contrasts the sweet spiciness of the sausage, a meaty richness that makes this dish incredibly satisfying and helps bring it alive on the tongue. You can experiment with your own favorite type of sausage. In any case, the sauce is a wonderfully light vehicle for the cacophony of savory flavors.

*1. Preheat a large sauté pan over medium-high heat. Add the olive oil. When the oil is hot, add the sausage and brown, breaking up the sausage into quarter-size pieces as it cooks.*

*2. Add the sliced garlic and sauté until it begins to pick up color. Add the broccoli rabe, roasted garlic, sun-dried tomatoes, 1 tablespoon of the basil, and 1½ teaspoons of the parsley and sauté for about 2 minutes.*

*3. Add the chicken stock and cook until the liquid has reduced by one-quarter. Finish the sauce with the remaining 1 tablespoon basil and 1½ teaspoons parsley, the salt, and pepper.*

*4. Add the cooked pasta and cheese to the pan and toss to coat. Serve in a medium serving bowl or on a deep platter, garnished with the toasted bread crumbs.*

# Perciatelli Amatriciana

*Serves 4 to 5*

¼ cup Garlic Oil (page 242)

4 ounces pancetta, julienned

1 cup sliced red onion

¼ cup sliced garlic

3 cloves Roasted Garlic (page 242)

⅛ teaspoon crushed red
pepper flakes

¾ cup red wine

24 ounces canned whole, peeled
Italian plum tomatoes

3 tablespoons chopped fresh basil

2 tablespoons chopped fresh flat-leaf
parsley

½ teaspoon kosher salt

⅛ teaspoon cracked black pepper

1 tablespoon unsalted butter

12 ounces perciatelli, cooked al dente

¾ cup grated Romano cheese

This dish is named for Amatrice, a town due east of Rome and justly famous for the chefs it produces. The secret of the dish is to infuse the tomato sauce with the essence of bacon, creating a blend of slightly acidic, garden-rich goodness embellished with down-to-earth salty pork flavor. We've coupled this delightful sauce with the equally delightful pasta, perciatelli, a distinctive spaghetti-like noodle with a hollow center—which essentially serves as straws that capture the sauce inside and out.

1. *Preheat a large sauté pan over medium-high heat. When hot, add the garlic oil and pancetta and sauté until browned.*

2. *Add the onions, garlics, and the red pepper flakes and sauté until the mixture begins to brown. Deglaze the pan with the red wine, scraping up any carmelized bits stuck to the bottom. Cook until the liquid has reduced by half.*

3. *Add the tomatoes and simmer for about 10 minutes, breaking up the whole tomatoes as they simmer.*

4. *Finish the sauce with the basil, parsley, salt, black pepper, and butter. Add the cooked pasta and grated cheese to the pan and toss to coat. Serve hot in a medium serving bowl or on a deep platter.*

# THE ITALIAN PANTRY: PASTA MADE SIMPLE

Italian kitchen creativity is most on display in the number of ways pasta has been used in traditional dishes. The choices can be divided, at the most basic level, into dried or fresh varieties. Fresh pasta is made with eggs and was traditionally the starch of choice in areas of the north, while dried versions made with water and flour enjoyed more popularity throughout the rest of the country. There is a place, a time, and a dish for both dried and fresh pastas.

## Dried or Fresh?

Americans entertain a fetish for fresh pasta, but fresh isn't necessarily better. In fact, in many instances, dried is preferable. To understand why, you need to understand what separates the two.

**Fresh pasta** is made from eggs, flour, and more water than is used in dried versions. It is more delicate and tender, both cooked and uncooked, and takes about half as long to cook as the dried equivalent. It also takes more fresh pasta to feed a crowd—about 1½ pounds for four people, where 1 pound of dried pasta will do the job.

**Dried pasta** can be stored longer, is more widely available, and usually costs less. But the real difference lies in the cooking. Fresh pastas are best suited to more delicate sauces and preparations or for use in broths and light soups. Heat and liquid saturation will quickly break down most fresh pastas, making dried pasta the clear choice in recipes like lasagna or baked ziti. Dried also hold up better to richer, chunkier, and thicker sauces. But this much is true: no matter which type you choose, the pasta must be cooked correctly.

## Perfectly Prepared Pasta

Cooking pasta perfectly begins with the water. One of the most common errors home cooks make is using too little water. A pound of pasta calls for 6 quarts (24 cups) of water. Pasta sheds starch as it cooks. Too little water means that the noodles will essentially stew in a starch broth, which can only lead to gummy, rubbery, unsatisfying pasta. Pasta water should be salted heavily, so that it "tastes like the sea," and should be brought to a rolling boil. And a word to the wise: never, ever add oil to your pasta water.

The next and the most critical aspect is time. Cook it too long, and you'll wind up with overly limp noodles. The ideal for any pasta is al dente, Italian for "to the tooth." It means that properly cooked pasta maintains a little resistance, almost a "snap" when bit. There is no substitute for constant testing. As the pasta cooks, pull out a noodle, cool it, and bite it. Do this regularly until the pasta is al dente. Then remove it immediately and drain.

Even the most carefully cooked pasta must be sauced correctly. When serving, sauce the pasta sparingly. If there is a puddle of sauce left on the plate after the pasta has been eaten, the cook has used too much sauce.

When you get comfortable with cooking pasta, you may want to try removing the pasta from the water right before it reaches the al dente stage, and finish cooking it in the pan of hot sauce. (Unless the directions call for dressing the pasta with the sauce on top.)

# Frutti di Mare over Linguini

*Serves 4 to 6*

¾ cup olive oil

2 tablespoons sliced garlic

3 cloves Roasted Garlic (page 242)

½ pound jumbo shrimp

¼ pound sea scallops

2 cups clam juice

3 tablespoons chopped fresh basil

2 tablespoons chopped fresh
flat-leaf parsley

12 Littleneck clams

12 PEI mussels (substitute local
varieties if PEI are not available)

10 ounces calamari, cut into
½-inch rings

½ teaspoon crushed red pepper
flakes

12 ounces linguini, cooked al dente

Carmine's flagship restaurant is located in the heart of Times Square. That's about dead center in New York City, a coastal town with widely available fresh seafood—including some spectacular shellfish. That's why we love to serve this dish to our guests; they can taste the best the Atlantic has to offer, married with simple linguini. Do honor to the many flavors by pairing this dish with a full-bodied white, such as a Fiano, or the briny Vermentino.

*1. Heat the oil in a large sauté pan over medium-high heat. Add the sliced garlic and sauté until lightly browned. Increase the heat to high and add the roasted garlic, shrimp, and scallops and sauté for 1 minute on each side. Remove and set aside.*

*2. Add the clam juice to the pan, and bring to a boil. Add 1½ tablespoons of the basil, 1 tablespoon of the parsley, and the clams and mussels. Reduce to a simmer and cover the pan. Cook, checking the shellfish every 1 to 2 minutes, and remove and set aside as they open. Discard any shellfish that do not open*

*3. Add the calamari to the pan and simmer for about 6 minutes, uncovered, until the sauce has reduced and the calamari is cooked through.*

*4. Return all of the seafood to the pan, along with the red pepper flakes and simmer for 2 minutes more.*

*5. To serve, place the hot cooked pasta in the center of a deep serving platter, arrange the mussels and clams around the outside, and top the pasta with the sauce and remaining seafood. Sprinkle the remaining basil and parsley over top and serve.*

# Farfalle with Chicken, Asparagus, and Mushrooms

*Serves 4 to 6*

¾ pound boneless, skinless chicken breast, cut into 1-inch pieces

1½ teaspoons kosher salt

¼ teaspoon cracked black pepper

¾ cup olive oil

½ cup sliced garlic

4 ounces crimini mushrooms, cleaned, stems trimmed

6 ounces white button mushrooms, cleaned, stems trimmed

2 ounces sun-dried tomatoes, julienned

1½ cups chopped (1-inch pieces) asparagus

½ cup Roasted Red Peppers (page 252)

2 tablespoons chopped fresh basil

1 tablespoon chopped fresh flat-leaf parsley

2 cups chicken stock

¾ cup grated Romano cheese

9 pitted black Ligurian olives (or substitute Niçoise olives)

12 ounces farfalle, cooked al dente

2 tablespoons Toasted Bread Crumbs (page 246)

Some pasta is simply fun. Farfalle is known as "bow-tie" pasta, with a shape that ensures a sturdy texture between the teeth and that really livens up the plate. More importantly, though, it has an abundance of nooks and crannies in which spices and flavors can hide. Pan-seared chicken, asparagus, and mushrooms all add intriguing textures to this multifaceted pasta dish.

*1. Dust the chicken with ¾ teaspoon of the salt and ⅛ teaspoon of the black pepper. Heat the olive oil in a large sauté pan over medium-high heat. When the oil is hot, add the chicken and sauté until browned. Remove the chicken and add the garlic, and sauté until browned. Add the mushrooms and sauté for about 2 minutes.*

*2. Add the sun-dried tomatoes, asparagus, roasted red peppers, 1 tablespoon of the basil, 1½ teaspoons of the parsley, and the remaining ¾ teaspoon salt and ⅛ teaspoon black pepper and cook for 3 minutes. Add the chicken stock and continue to cook until the liquid has reduced by half.*

*3. Finish the sauce with the remaining 1 tablespoon basil, the remaining 1½ teaspoons parsley, the grated cheese, and the black olives. Add the cooked pasta to the sauce and toss to coat. Serve in a large serving bowl or on a deep platter, garnished with the toasted bread crumbs.*

# Pasta Carbonara

*Serves 4 to 5*

3 ounces pancetta, finely diced

3 slices thick-cut bacon

1 tablespoon chopped garlic

1 tablespoon chopped shallots

3 tablespoons chopped fresh basil

2 tablespoons chopped fresh
flat-leaf parsley

1 pint heavy cream

$^3/_4$ teaspoon kosher salt

$^1/_4$ teaspoon cracked black pepper

1 egg yolk, beaten

$^3/_4$ cup grated Romano cheese

1 tablespoon unsalted butter

12 ounces perciatelli, cooked al dente

This wonderful, rich and filling dish is said to have originated as the main meal of *carbonaio*, men who would spend weeks at a time in the forest, making charcoal in the traditional fashion. It was a hard life, and they needed an all-in-one meal that would be substantial and—being Italian—absolutely delicious. Eggs and cheese make a full-bodied sauce that clings to the hollow spaghetti relative, perciatelli. A dose of pancetta makes this essentially the bacon-and-eggs pasta with the power to soothe a weary soul.

*1. Preheat a large sauté pan over medium-high heat. Add the pancetta and cook for 2 minutes. Add the bacon and cook until both meats are browned and crisp. Transfer to a paper towel–lined plate and set aside.*

*2. Reserve about half of the rendered fat from the bacon and pancetta (discard the rest). Add the garlic and shallots to the pan and sauté until they begin to pick up some color. Add 1½ tablespoons of the basil and 1 tablespoon of the parsley and sauté for 30 seconds.*

*3. Add the heavy cream, salt, and pepper and cook until the liquid has reduced by half. At that point, reduce the temperature to medium and return the bacon and pancetta to the pan, reserving a small portion for garnish. Remove from the heat and whisk in the egg yolk.*

*4. When the yolk is completely incorporated, fold in the cheese, the remaining 1½ tablespoons basil, the remaining 1 tablespoon parsley, and the butter. Add the cooked pasta and toss until well coated. Transfer to a large serving platter and garnish with the reserved bacon and pancetta just before serving.*

# Shrimp alla Roma

*Serves 4 to 6*

1¹/₂ pounds jumbo shrimp

30 ounces canned whole, peeled Italian plum tomatoes

1³/₄ cups extra-virgin olive oil

Two 8-ounce bottles clam juice

1¹/₂ pounds Beefsteak tomatoes

¹/₂ cup julienned red onion

2 tablespoons chopped fresh flat-leaf parsley

¹/₂ cup chopped fresh basil

1 tablespoon chopped garlic

1 teaspoon kosher salt

¹/₄ teaspoon crushed red pepper flakes

12 ounces spaghetti, cooked al dente

The delicate sweetness of the shrimp in this dish is perfectly cut by the hearty full flavor of the tomatoes. The dish is accented by just a scattering of a few traditional spices and herbs, and wants for nothing else. It's a treat on the tongue that delivers a little burst of shellfish in almost every bite, with a sturdy sauce that coats the pasta and provides an ample stage for the seafood.

*1. Peel, devein, and clean the shrimp. Reserve the shells and tails. In a small bowl, lightly crush one-third of the canned tomatoes. In a small pot over medium heat, combine the olive oil, shrimp shells, and crushed tomatoes and simmer for 1 hour.*

*2. Strain the sauce through a chinois (a conical fine-mesh sieve), or use a regular sieve lined with cheesecloth, pressing the shells and tomatoes to extract all of the oil.*

*3. In a separate small pot over medium-high heat, combine the sieved oil with the remaining canned tomatoes and bring to a boil. Reduce to a simmer and cook for about 15 minutes.*

*4. In a third small pot over medium-high heat, bring the clam juice to a boil. Add the shrimp, and boil for about 2½ minutes, or until the shrimp are pink and firm. Remove and set aside.*

*5. Continue boiling the clam juice until it has reduced to ¼ cup of liquid, then add it to the pot with the canned tomatoes.*

*6. Core the beefsteak tomatoes and gently score a small X in the bottom of each tomato, cutting just through the skin. In a small stockpot over medium-high heat, bring 8 cups of water to a boil. Fill a large heatproof bowl halfway with water and fill it the rest of the way with ice. Set the ice bath aside.*

7. Boil the tomatoes for 30 to 45 seconds, or just until you notice the skin beginning to peel back from the scored mark. Transfer the tomatoes to the ice bath to stop the cooking process. After about 3 minutes, remove the tomatoes and gently peel and discard the skins. Cut each tomato into eight sections and squeeze gently to remove the seeds.

8. In a large bowl, combine the beefsteak tomatoes, onions, parsley, basil, garlic, salt, red pepper flakes, and the canned tomato mixture. Slice the shrimp in half lengthwise and add to the bowl. Set aside for 15 minutes, to allow the flavors to meld.

9. Spread out the cooked, hot pasta in the center of an oval serving platter. Pour the sauce over top, and arrange the beefsteak tomatoes and shrimp around the edges just before serving.

# Capellini Marechiara

*Serves 4 to 6*

3/4 cup Garlic Oil (page 242)

1/4 cup sliced garlic

1/2 pound jumbo shrimp

1/4 pound sea scallops

2 cups clam juice

4 cloves Roasted Garlic (page 242)

1/4 cup finely diced hot Italian peppers

3 tablespoons chopped fresh basil

1 tablespoon chopped fresh flat-leaf parsley

8 Littleneck clams

8 PEI mussels (substitute a local variety if PEI are not available)

8 ounces canned whole, peeled Italian plum tomatoes

1/4 teaspoon salt

1/8 teaspoon freshly ground black pepper

1 cup packed arugula leaves, rinsed, stems trimmed

3/4 pound capellini, cooked al dente

If there is one supreme lesson of Italian cooking, it's that most times, simple is best. That's the principle behind this uncomplicated union of garlic and tomatoes, olive oil and white wine. The balance of the ingredients is what makes the sauce magic on any seafood. We've coupled the sauce with capellini, better known as angel hair pasta. It just naturally complements the fresh lively elements in the dish.

*1. Heat the garlic oil in a large sauté pan over medium-high heat. Add the sliced garlic and brown slightly. Add the shrimp and scallops, increase the heat to high, and sauté for 1 minute on each side. Remove the seafood and set aside.*

*2. Add the clam juice and reduce the heat to a simmer. Add the roasted garlic, hot peppers, basil, parsley, clams, and mussels, cover, and bring to a boil. Cook, checking every 1 to 2 minutes, and as the shellfish open remove and set aside with the shrimp and scallops. Discard any shellfish that do not open.*

*3. Uncover and add the plum tomatoes, salt, and black pepper to the broth in the pan. Cook on high until the liquid has reduced by about one-quarter, 3 to 5 minutes.*

*4. Cook the pasta. Return all of the seafood to the pan, simmer for 1 minute. Add the arugula and cook for 1 minute more, or just until the arugula wilts.*

*5. Spread the hot cooked pasta in the center of a large serving platter. Top the pasta with the sauce, arrange the clams and mussels around the outside edges, and serve.*

# Pasta Quattro Formaggi

*Serves 4 to 6*

1 tablespoon unsalted butter

1 teaspoon chopped shallots

2 teaspoons chiffonade of fresh sage

$1/4$ cup white wine

$1^1/_2$ cups heavy cream

1 cup chicken stock

$1/2$ teaspoon kosher salt

$1/8$ teaspoon cracked black pepper

Two 14-ounce packages frozen gnocchi

$1/3$ cup grated Asiago cheese

$1/4$ cup finely diced fresh mozzarella cheese

$1/4$ cup grated Grana Padano cheese

$1/2$ cup shredded fontina cheese

1 teaspoon chopped fresh flat-leaf parsley

In Italian opera, the saying goes: "If one tenor is good, four tenors can only be better." At Carmine's we paraphrase: "If one cheese teases the palate, four will be a taste of heaven." Although you can certainly choose the quartet that appeals to you, Carmine's chefs intentionally chose these four because they complement each other and offer something for all the parts of the tongue—sweet, tart, strong, subtle, nutty, and beyond

*1. Preheat a large sauté pan over medium-high heat. Combine the butter and shallots in the pan and sauté for 2 minutes. Add 1 teaspoon of the sage and all the white wine and cook until the liquid has reduced by half.*

*2. Add the cream, chicken stock, salt, and pepper. Cook until the liquid has again reduced by half.*

*3. Cook the gnocchi according to the package directions. Whisk the four cheeses into the sauce. Add the gnocchi and toss to coat. Taste and add salt and pepper as necessary. Serve on serving platter and garnish with the remaining 1 teaspoon sage and the chopped parsley sprinkled over the top.*

# Pasta with Roasted Eggplant and Mozzarella

*Serves 4 to 6*

1 cup olive oil

³/₄ teaspoon kosher salt

¹/₄ teaspoon cracked black pepper

1¹/₄ pounds eggplant, cut into 1¹/₂-inch wedges

¹/₄ cup sliced garlic

2 ounces pancetta, julienned

4 cloves Roasted Garlic (page 242)

1 cup julienned red onion

4 tablespoons chopped fresh basil

3 tablespoons chopped fresh flat-leaf parsley

¹/₄ cup white wine

One 28-ounce can whole, peeled Italian plum tomatoes

12 ounces penne, cooked al dente

3 tablespoons grated Romano cheese

2 ounces oil-cured black olives, pitted and halved

6 ounces fresh mozzarella cheese, cut into 1-inch cubes

Eggplant and mozzarella are incredibly compatible, especially when the cheese is not totally melted and the eggplant is cut a bit coarse. The chunky ingredients in the sauce and topping work with the tubular penne pasta to create a rustic feel—making a dish that would be right at home on a Tuscan farmhouse table.

1. *Preheat the oven to 400°F.*

2. *In a medium bowl, whisk together ¼ cup of the olive oil, ½ teaspoon of the salt, and ⅛ teaspoon of the pepper. Lightly coat the eggplant with this mixture. Spread the eggplant out on a sheet pan and roast for 15 to 20 minutes, until evenly browned. Remove from the oven and let cool to room temperature.*

3. *In a large sauté pan over medium-high heat, heat the remaining ¾ cup olive oil. Add the sliced garlic and pancetta and sauté until browned. Add the roasted garlic, onion, basil, and parsley and sauté for 2 minutes, or until the onions become translucent.*

4. *Add the wine and cook for about 2 minutes. Add the tomatoes and cook for 10 minutes more.*

5. *Cook the pasta. Add the remaining ¼ teaspoon salt and ⅛ teaspoon pepper, Romano cheese, and olives to the pan of tomato sauce. Add the hot, drained pasta to the sauce and toss to coat well. Fold in the mozzarella and spread out on a serving platter.*

6. *Arrange the roasted eggplant wedges on top of the pasta, garnish with the parsley, and serve.*

# Penne alla Boscaiola

*Serves 4 to 6*

³/₄ cup Garlic Oil (page 242)

¹/₂ pound bulk sweet Italian sausage

1¹/₂ cups sliced white onions

¹/₂ teaspoon crushed red pepper flakes

3 ounces spicy sopressata, julienned

¹/₄ cup sliced garlic

3 tablespoons chopped fresh basil

2 tablespoons chopped fresh flat-leaf parsley

9 ounces white button mushrooms, cleaned, stems trimmed, thickly sliced

20 ounces canned whole, peeled Italian plum tomatoes

1 cup heavy cream

12 ounces penne, cooked al dente

1 cup grated Romano cheese

The term *alla boscaiola* translates to "in the style of the woodsman"; it makes sense once you fill a plate with all the rustic goodness of tube pasta threading through a cascade of mushrooms and rugged herbs. Peasants in the south of Italy traditionally turned to the forest for many cooking ingredients, and it's easy to see how this dish came together from a day spent foraging.

*1. Heat the garlic oil in a large sauté pan over medium-high heat. When the oil is hot, add the sausage and brown, breaking it into quarter-size pieces as you cook.*

*2. Add the onions, red pepper flakes, sopressata, and sliced garlic to the pan. When the garlic begins to brown, add 1½ tablespoons of the basil and 1 tablespoon of the parsley. Add the mushrooms and sauté for about 2 minutes.*

*3. Add the tomatoes and cream and cook until the liquid has reduced by one-quarter, breaking up the whole tomatoes as they simmer.*

*4. Cook the pasta. Finish the sauce with the remaining 1½ tablespoons basil, the remaining 1 tablespoon parsley, and the grated cheese. Add the hot pasta to the sauce and toss to coat. Serve in a medium bowl or on a deep platter.*

# Spaghetti with Carmine's Meatballs

*Serves 6 to 8*

1½ cups Carmine's Bread Crumbs (page 244)

2½ cups chicken stock

1½ tablespoons chopped garlic

2 large eggs, beaten

4 tablespoons chopped fresh flat-leaf parsley

4 tablespoons chopped fresh basil

1 tablespoon kosher salt

½ teaspoon freshly ground black pepper

½ pound ground veal

1½ pounds fresh ground beef chuck (80 percent lean)

1¼ cups grated Romano cheese

10 cups Carmine's Marinara Sauce (page 251)

2 pounds spaghetti, cooked al dente

Every restaurant has its signature dish, and this lovely affair is ours. Subtly spiced meatballs are the very definition of comfort food, and perfectly cooked spaghetti is the best friend any meatballs could ask for. We make our meatballs from a combination of fresh ground chuck (not prepackaged meat) with a portion of veal. This adds just a bit of sweetness to the mix and, along with the other ingredients, makes the flavor a little more complex than the average meatball.

*1. Preheat the oven to 450°F.*

*2. In a large bowl, combine the bread crumbs, 1 cup of the chicken stock, the garlic, eggs, 3 tablespoons of the parsley, 2 tablespoons of the basil, the salt, and pepper. Add the veal, beef, and 1 cup of the grated cheese. Using your hands, mix well, but do not overwork the mixture. Refrigerate for 1 hour to allow the mixture to set up.*

*3. Lightly oil a high-sided sheet pan with olive oil. Using a large ice cream scoop, scoop out rounded balls of the meat mixture. Arrange them on the sheet pan, spacing the balls evenly apart, until you've used up the mixture; there should be about 12 balls.*

*4. Coat your hands with a little bit of olive oil and tightly pack each ball while rolling it round to maintain a uniform shape.*

*5. Pour the remaining 1½ cups of chicken stock into the sheet pan around the meatballs. Bake for 15 to 20 minutes, or until the meatballs are browned and cooked through. Remove and let cool.*

*6. When you're ready to serve, combine the meatballs with the* marinara sauce in a medium pot, and simmer for 15 to 20 minutes. While the meatballs simmer, cook the spaghetti.

7. Spread the pasta out on a serving platter and place half the meatballs along the center. Top with 3 cups of the sauce. Garnish with 2 tablespoons of the grated cheese, the remaining 1 tablespoon parsley, and 1 tablespoon of the basil, and serve.

8. Add the remaining 2 tablespoons cheese and 1 tablespoon basil to the remaining sauce and meatballs.

9. Let any leftover meatballs and sauce cool and then refrigerate for meatball heroes the next day.

# Lasagna, Vegetarian-Style

*Serves 8 to 10 (one half hotel pan)*

**EGG BATTER**

8 extra-large eggs

1/3 cup grated Romano cheese

1/4 cup chopped fresh flat-leaf parsley

1/4 teaspoon kosher salt

1/4 teaspoon cracked black pepper

**MUSHROOM FILLING**

3 tablespoons olive oil

1 1/2 teaspoons chopped garlic

1 pound crimini mushrooms, cleaned, stems trimmed, sliced

2 tablespoons chopped fresh basil

1/2 teaspoon kosher salt

1/4 teaspoon cracked black pepper

**SPINACH FILLING**

3 tablespoons olive oil

1 teaspoon chopped garlic

1/2 pound spinach leaves, well rinsed and dried

1/4 teaspoon kosher salt

1/4 teaspoon cracked pepper

**CHEESE FILLING**

1 1/2 pounds whole-milk ricotta cheese

1 extra-large egg

1/4 cup grated Romano cheese

At Carmine's, we like to accommodate different preferences and tastes. So, for the non–meat eaters in the crowd, we offer this magnificent lasagna. We fill it with a wholesome blend of garden-fresh ingredients and bring it all together with our own special luscious marinara. The blend of veggies provides just the right tumble of textures to contrast the smooth cheesiness of the recipe.

**TO MAKE THE BATTER**

*In a medium bowl, whisk together all the ingredients for the egg batter. Set aside.*

**TO MAKE THE MUSHROOM FILLING**

*Heat the olive oil in a large sauté pan over medium-high heat. Add the garlic. When the garlic begins to brown, add the mushrooms and basil and sauté over high heat until the mushrooms pick up color and start to become tender. Sprinkle with the salt and pepper, transfer to a plate and let cool.*

**TO MAKE THE SPINACH FILLING**

*Heat the olive oil in a large sauté pan over medium-high heat. Add the garlic. When it begins to brown, add the spinach. Increase the heat to high, and sauté for 30 seconds. Sprinkle with the salt and black pepper. Transfer to a plate, and let cool. Squeeze and drain out any extra liquid.*

**TO MAKE THE CHEESE FILLING**

*In a medium bowl, mix together all the ingredients. Refrigerate until ready to use.*

¼ cup chopped fresh flat-leaf parsley

½ teaspoon kosher salt

¼ teaspoon cracked black pepper

**EGGPLANT AND ZUCCHINI**

2 cups canola oil, for frying

½ pound all-purpose flour

¾ pound eggplant, ends trimmed, cut lengthwise into ⅜-inch-thick slices

¾ pound large zucchini, ends trimmed, cut lengthwise into ⅜-inch-thick slices

**LASAGNA**

3¾ cups Carmine's Marinara Sauce (page 251)

1 pound lasagna noodles, parboiled in salted water for 8 minutes

1 pound whole milk mozzarella cheese, shredded

¾ cup grated Romano cheese

½ cup Roasted Red Peppers (page 252)

4 tablespoons chopped fresh basil leaves

**TO MAKE THE EGGPLANT AND ZUCCHINI**

*1. Heat a large, high-sided pan or skillet filled with 1½ inches of canola oil, until the oil reaches 325°F. While the oil is heating, set up a breading station next to the skillet. Fill a shallow pan with the egg batter, and another shallow pan with the flour. Line a sheet pan with several layers of paper towels.*

*2. Dust two to three pieces of eggplant in the flour, coating both sides. Shake off the excess. Using tongs, dip the pieces in the egg batter and then slide them into the hot oil. Fry for about 1 minute each side, or until nicely browned all over. Transfer the pieces to the paper towel–lined sheet pan and pat the tops of the vegetables dry with more paper towels.*

*3. Continue battering and frying the eggplant and zucchini, being careful not to crowd the pan. When all the vegetables have been fried and patted dry, refrigerate to cool.*

**TO ASSEMBLE THE LASAGNE**

*1. Preheat the oven to 350°F.*

*2. Build the lasagna in a half hotel pan (12¾ x 10½ x 4 inches), working from the bottom up, according to the following pattern:*

- *Spread 1 cup of the marinara over the bottom of the pan*
- *Layer in 4 lasagna noodles*
- *Layer half of the fried eggplant slices*
- *Spread over ¾ cup of the marinara sauce*
- *Sprinkle over one-quarter of the shredded mozzarella, and 2 tablespoons of the grated Romano*
- *Spread a layer of the cheese filling*

*(continued)*

- *Layer in 4 lasagna noodles, and press down with the spatula*
- *Layer in half of the zucchini slices*
- *Spread over ¾ cup of the marinara*
- *Spread the drained mushroom filling, topped with the drained spinach filling and the roasted peppers*
- *Sprinkle over one-quarter of the shredded mozzarella, and 2 tablespoons of the grated Romano*
- *Spread on a layer of the cheese filling*
- *Layer in 4 lasagna noodles, and press down all over with a spatula*
- *Sprinkle over one-quarter of the shredded mozzarella, and 2 tablespoons of the grated Romano*
- *Layer half the remaining zucchini mixed with half the remaining eggplant*
- *Layer in a mixture of 1 cup of the ricotta filling, 2 tablespoons Romano, and 2 tablespoons chopped basil*
- *Layer the remaining 4 lasagna noodles and press down with the spatula*
- *Spread over the remaining ¾ cup marinara*
- *Top with a mixture of one-quarter of the mozzarella and 2 tablespoons of the Romano cheese*

*3. Cover the pan with plastic wrap, then cover with a layer of aluminum foil. Bake for 1 hour, or until hot all the way through and the cheese has nicely melted.*

*4. Tightly wrap up any leftovers after they have cooled completely, and keep in the refrigerator for up to a week, and in the freezer for up to 2 months.*

# Lamb Bolognese with Fresh Ricotta

*Serves 4 to 6*

1/2 cup olive oil

1/2 cup finely chopped carrots

1/2 cup finely chopped celery

1/2 cup finely chopped white onions

1 1/2 tablespoons sliced garlic

1 1/2 pounds fresh ground lamb
  (cut from the leg)

1 teaspoon kosher salt

1/4 teaspoon cracked pepper

1 1/2 teaspoons chopped fresh
  rosemary

1 teaspoon chopped fresh oregano

1 tablespoon chopped fresh flat-leaf
  parsley

1 tablespoon chopped fresh basil

2 bay leaves

1/2 cup red wine

2 1/2 cups canned whole, peeled plum
  tomatoes, with their juices

1/3 cup plus 1 tablespoon grated
  Romano cheese

12 ounces pappardelle, cooked
  al dente

1 cup fresh whole-milk ricotta cheese

*Bolognese* was one of the original Italian meat sauces, traditionally called *Ragu alla Bolognese*. We use lamb with our version to add a hint of sweetness and a bit more delicate flavor. The sauce is often paired with broad noodles such as pappardelle, or hollow pasta like the penne shown here. In either case, a maximum of pasta surface helps you capture all of this sturdy sauce.

*1. Heat 1/4 cup of the olive oil in a large sauté pan over high heat. Add the carrots, celery, onions, and garlic and sauté until the vegetables brown.*

*2. In a separate large sauté pan over high heat, heat the remaining 1/4 cup olive oil. Add the ground lamb, breaking up the meat into medium-size pieces as you brown it. (Leave the pieces of lamb in one spot in the pan, and when browned, flip each piece over and brown the opposite side.) Add the salt and pepper, 1 teaspoon of the rosemary, the oregano, parsley, basil, and bay leaves and mix well to combine.*

*3. Combine the lamb with the sautéed vegetables. Add the red wine and cook until the liquid has reduced by half. Add the tomatoes and simmer for 30 minutes, breaking them up as they cook.*

*4. Add 1/3 cup of the Romano cheese. Transfer the cooked pasta in a medium bowl or on a deep serving platter, and cover with the sauce. Garnish with dollops of the ricotta, the remaining 1 tablespoon Romano cheese, and remaining 1/2 teaspoon rosemary.*

# Fish and Seafood

When your front yard is the sea, you make the most of the bounty that is there for the taking. The expansive coastline of the Italian peninsula, along with the islands of Sicily and Sardinia, has always translated to great fishing and an incredible diversity of seafood in Italian dishes. It has also been a way of cleaving to the rules of religion while still satisfying the desires of the palate. Until the mid-1960s, the Roman Catholic Church required that the faithful eat fish rather than meat on Fridays—and, in some cases, Wednesdays and Saturdays—as well as other holy days. Italian cooks turned that stricture into a reason to celebrate the culinary glories of the Mediterranean—their "fruit of the sea."

Seafood was also the most readily available protein to the more impoverished households in Southern Italy. That's why many of the everyday classic seafood recipes come out of the South and, in the spirit of waste not, want not, those recipes include just about anything that can be harvested from the sea. Whole fish, fillets, shellfish, and even slippery squid and octopus found their way into Old World recipes. We pay appropriate homage to that tradition at Carmine's by serving a mouthwatering diversity of seafood dishes.

Delectable seafood is a natural partner for all the other constituents of Italian cooking. Almost everything the fisherman brings to port marries incredibly well with simple sauces of olive oil and garlic, and heavier preparations of tomatoes, herbs, and cheese. Pull in your own catch of the day, and see what magic you can make with the fruit of the sea.

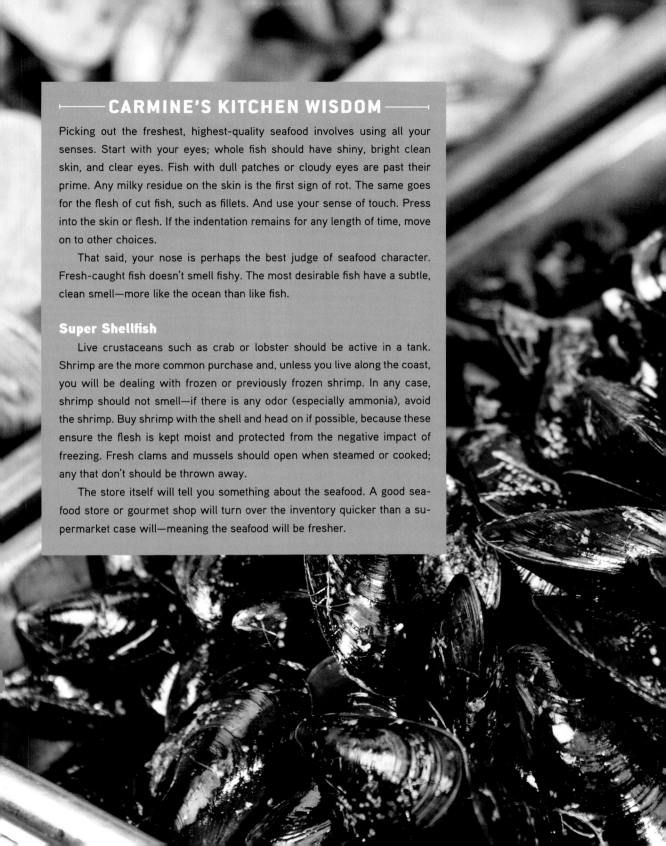

## ┤ CARMINE'S KITCHEN WISDOM ├

Picking out the freshest, highest-quality seafood involves using all your senses. Start with your eyes; whole fish should have shiny, bright clean skin, and clear eyes. Fish with dull patches or cloudy eyes are past their prime. Any milky residue on the skin is the first sign of rot. The same goes for the flesh of cut fish, such as fillets. And use your sense of touch. Press into the skin or flesh. If the indentation remains for any length of time, move on to other choices.

That said, your nose is perhaps the best judge of seafood character. Fresh-caught fish doesn't smell fishy. The most desirable fish have a subtle, clean smell—more like the ocean than like fish.

### Super Shellfish

Live crustaceans such as crab or lobster should be active in a tank. Shrimp are the more common purchase and, unless you live along the coast, you will be dealing with frozen or previously frozen shrimp. In any case, shrimp should not smell—if there is any odor (especially ammonia), avoid the shrimp. Buy shrimp with the shell and head on if possible, because these ensure the flesh is kept moist and protected from the negative impact of freezing. Fresh clams and mussels should open when steamed or cooked; any that don't should be thrown away.

The store itself will tell you something about the seafood. A good seafood store or gourmet shop will turn over the inventory quicker than a supermarket case will—meaning the seafood will be fresher.

# Sea Bass Cioppino

*Serves 4 to 6*

- ³/₄ cup olive oil blend (3 parts canola oil to 1 part olive oil)

- 1¹/₂ pounds skinless, boneless Chilean sea bass, center cut, butterflied

- 1¹/₂ teaspoons kosher salt

- ³/₈ teaspoons ground white pepper

- ¹/₂ pound extra-large shrimp, shelled and deveined

- ¹/₂ pound dry-packed jumbo scallops, side muscle removed

- 12 Littleneck clams, cleaned

- 12 PEI mussels (substitute a local variety if PEI are not available), cleaned

- 2 tablespoons thinly sliced garlic

- 1 cup thinly sliced celery

- 1 cup cored and thinly sliced fennel

- 4 tablespoons chopped fresh basil

- 4 tablespoons chopped fresh flat-leaf parsley

- ¹/₂ teaspoon saffron

- 1 large dried bay leaf

- ¹/₂ cup white wine

- 1 tablespoon fennel seed

- 3¹/₄ cups clam juice

- 1³/₄ cups canned whole, peeled Italian plum tomatoes

Every culture with a coastline has some form of seafood stew, a hearty mix that the fisherman boils up right on the boat. Cioppino is a great example of a filling fisherman's stew, an Italian-American dish, developed in San Francisco in the early twentieth century. We include naturally sweet shell-fish with a distinctive sea bass that creates a wonderfully vi-brant undertone to the stew. The combination of basic herbs, spices, and tomatoes makes for a hearty foundation, creating the perfect hearty dinner to chase the cold out of your bones.

*1. Heat 6 tablespoons of the olive oil in a large sauté pan over medium-high heat. Season the sea bass with ¹/₂ teaspoon of the salt and ³/₈ teaspoon of the pepper. Gently slide the fish into the pan and brown each side, but do not fully cook the fish. Set aside.*

*2. Repeat this process to cook the shrimp and scallops, seasoning them before cooking with ¹/₂ teaspoon salt and ¹/₈ teaspoon pep-per. Set aside.*

*3. Add the remaining 6 tablespoons olive oil to the pan and sauté the garlic until lightly browned. Add the celery, sliced fennel, 2 tablespoons each of the basil and parsley, the saffron, and the bay leaf. Reduce the heat to medium and cook until the vegetables are just a bit tender and begin sweating.*

*4. Add the white wine and fennel seed and cook until the liquid has reduced by half.*

*5. Add the clam juice, tomatoes, the remaining ¹/₂ teaspoon salt, and ¹/₈ teaspoon pepper and bring the sauce to a boil. Add the clams and mussels and cover with a lid. Check often and, as each* one opens, remove and set aside until all of the clams and mussels are cooked; discard any that do not open.

6. Increase the heat to high, and cook until the sauce has reduced by about 40 percent, about 15 minutes.

7. Carefully return the sea bass to the pan and simmer for 3 to 4 minutes, or until just cooked through. Transfer the fish to a serving platter.

8. Return the mussels, clams, shrimp, and scallops to the pan and cook for 1 minute. Place the shrimp and scallops on a platter along with the sea bass, and pour the sauce and shellfish on top of the bass. Sprinkle basil and parsley over top and serve.

# Sole Francese

*Serves 2 to 4*

4 to 5 large fingerling potatoes

8 ounces crimini or oyster mushrooms, cleaned, stems trimmed

2 tablespoons olive oil

Kosher salt

Freshly ground black pepper

Two 9-ounce fillets of sole

1 cup all-purpose flour

3 large eggs

3 tablespoons grated Romano cheese

2 tablespoons finely chopped fresh flat-leaf parsley

1/2 cup canola oil

8 tablespoons (1 stick) unsalted butter

2 tablespoons finely chopped shallots

1/4 cup dry white wine

1 1/2 cups clam juice

Juice of 2 lemons

1/2 pound dry-packed jumbo shrimp, peeled, deveined, and sliced diagonally

This recipe centers on a pan-fried fish fillet that boasts an appealingly delicate crunch on the outside, and perfectly cooked white fish on the inside. We include a scattering of delicious mushrooms and potatoes along with a scintillating white wine and butter sauce. When pan-frying any fish fillet such as this, handle it as little as possible. A big part of this dish is the elegant and impressive presentation, and a crumbled fish is less then attractive.

*1. Preheat the oven to 400°F.*

*2. Place the potatoes in a large saucepan, and add enough cold water to cover them by about 1 inch. Bring to a boil over medium-high heat. Reduce the heat and simmer for about 10 minutes, or until the potatoes are fork-tender.*

*3. Drain the potatoes and refrigerate until cool. Cut the potatoes in half lengthwise. Lay the halves, cut side up, in a single layer on a baking sheet and set aside.*

*4. In a bowl, toss the mushrooms with the olive oil and season them to taste with salt and pepper. Spread them out in a single layer on a baking sheet. Roast for 15 to 20 minutes, or until they are slightly dried and tender. Remove from the oven and set aside.*

*5. Reduce the oven temperature to 300°F. Line a plate with paper towels.*

*6. Season the sole with salt and pepper. Spread the flour on a plate. In a shallow bowl, whisk together the eggs, grated cheese, and 1 tablespoon of the parsley.*

*(continued)*

## Sole Francese *(continued)*

*7. Heat the canola oil in a large sauté pan over medium heat.*

*8. Coat the sole fillets with flour and shake off any excess. Dip the sole in the egg mixture and let any excess drip off. Carefully place the fish in the pan. Increase the heat to medium-high and cook it for about 3 minutes, or until golden brown. Gently shake the pan from time to time to prevent the fish from sticking. Carefully flip the fish and cook for about 3 minutes, or until it is golden brown on both sides and cooked through. Transfer to the paper towel–lined plate, and then transfer to a baking sheet.*

*9. Discard any oil from the sauté pan and wipe it clean with paper towels. Melt 1 teaspoon of the butter in the pan over medium heat. Add the shallots and cook, stirring occasionally, for 2 to 3 minutes, or until lightly browned.*

*10. Add the wine and cook with the shallots for 30 seconds. Add the clam juice, increase the heat to high, and bring the sauce to a boil. Boil for 3 to 4 minutes, or until the liquid has reduced by half. Reduce the heat to low and whisk in the remaining butter, 1 tablespoon at a time, until incorporated. Adjust the heat to maintain a simmer.*

*11. Add the lemon juice and shrimp to the sauce and season it to taste with salt and pepper. Simmer for 2 minutes, or until the shrimp are pink and cooked through. Stir in the remaining 1 tablespoon parsley.*

*12. Meanwhile, reheat the potatoes, mushrooms, and fish in the oven for about 5 minutes, or until heated through. Place the fish in the center of a platter. Arrange the potatoes around the fish and spread the mushrooms on top. Spoon the sauce over the sole and serve.*

You have only to smell garlic sizzling in hot olive oil, or taste the sweet, creamy essence of roasted garlic, to understand why this herb occupies such a central place in Italian cuisine.

It finds its way into antipasti, entrées, desserts, and even drinks. In fact, garlic complements everything from fish to pork, tomatoes to cheese. Still, more is not necessarily better; Italians use it often but sparingly, exercising the same balance and thoughtfulness they bring to all ingredients.

Before you begin peeling and chopping, you'll need to choose from among the hundreds of varieties. Only two types of the species *allium sativum* are regularly used as culinary garlic: softneck and hardneck. The aptly named "silverskin" variety of softneck garlic is the most universally available. It is so popular because it splits the difference between the more powerful wild garlic and the more moderate "weed" garlics.

Hardneck garlic is distinguished by a signature long, thick, sturdy stalk that runs right through the center of the bulb. Hardneck varieties such as Rocambole are prized for deep, full, rich flavors. The hardneck Purple Stripe garlic is a favorite for roasting.

## Buying the Right Bulb

Getting the best flavor out of any bulb of garlic means buying the freshest you can find. Look for firm bulbs with no soft spots or obvious rot or discoloration. Softneck varieties should have layers of papery "sheath" protecting the cloves and forming a tight bulb. Avoid bulbs that show any green growth or exposed cloves. The bulb shouldn't have any discernible odor.

## Pantry Garlic

Although a garlic braid can be a wonderful accent to your kitchen decor, any garlic you keep on hand should be as fresh as possible. Ideally, buy what you need on a weekly basis, using all the garlic you have on hand.

Avoid jarred, minced garlic. The surface areas are exposed to air, which quickly degrades the flavor. It isn't wise to infuse oil with cut garlic, because garlic stored in oil has been found to harbor botulism toxins. If you want to make use of extra garlic before it begins to dry out, roast it. You'll find our recipe for that kitchen staple on page 242.

# Stuffed Salmon

*Serves 4 to 6*

One 22-ounce salmon fillet, center cut, pin bones removed

1 teaspoon kosher salt

¼ teaspoon cracked black pepper

½ cup extra-virgin olive oil

2 tablespoons thinly sliced garlic

¼ cup finely diced red bell pepper

¼ cup finely diced celery

3 tablespoons chopped fresh basil

3 tablespoons chopped fresh flat-leaf parsley

¼ pound spinach leaves, well rinsed and sliced into thin strips

½ cup thinly sliced green onions, green part only

¼ cup white wine

2½ cups clam juice

4 ounces dry-packed jumbo sea scallops, trimmed of side muscle, quartered

4 ounces large shrimp, shelled, deveined, and quartered

1½ cups Carmine's Bread Crumbs (page 244)

1 tablespoon fresh lemon juice

2 ounces lump blue crabmeat

When a Carmine's guest is absolutely craving the total seafood experience, this is the dish we recommend. It combines the garden and the reef in a stuffing that is satisfying on every level possible. The scallops and shrimp make this a rich meal-in-one that is best complemented by a simple salad or vegetarian antipasti. Pair this dish with a big, full white like a Chardonnay or a rosé or a low-tannin, light-bodied red like a Pinot Nero or Dolcetto.

*1. Cut a pocket in the top of the salmon fillet. Season the fillet with ½ teaspoon of the kosher salt and all of the black pepper. Wrap it in plastic wrap and refrigerate until ready to cook.*

*2. Preheat the oven to 350°F.*

*3. Heat ¼ cup of the olive oil in a large sauté pan over medium-high heat. Add the garlic, bell pepper, celery, basil, and 2 tablespoons of the parsley and sauté until the vegetables are tender and lightly browned.*

*4. Add the spinach and green onions and cook for 1 minute more. Add the wine and ¼ cup of the clam juice and cook until the liquid has reduced by half. Add the scallops and shrimp and simmer for 2 minutes.*

*5. Remove the pan from the heat and fold in half of the bread crumbs, the lemon juice, and the remaining ½ teaspoon salt.*

*6. Transfer the shrimp mixture to a shallow pan, spread out evenly across the pan, and refrigerate until cool. When cool, remove the shrimp filling and the salmon from the refrigerator.*

7. *Lightly grease a small roasting pan. Stuff the pocket in the salmon fillet with the filling, and press the crabmeat in on top of the filling. Place the salmon into the pan and sprinkle the remaining bread crumbs on top, allowing a portion to drop off onto the pan. Drizzle with the remaining ¼ cup olive oil. Pour the remaining 2¼ cups clam juice around the salmon and cover the pan with aluminum foil.*

8. *Bake the salmon for 15 minutes. Remove the foil and bake for 15 to 20 minutes more, or until the breading is golden brown. The salmon should be cooked to medium and the filling should be hot.*

9. *Center the fish on a serving platter and pour the sauce around the dish. Garnish with the remaining 1 tablespoon parsley and serve.*

# Mussels Fra Diavolo

*Serves 4 to 6*

1/2 cup extra-virgin olive oil

2 tablespoons thinly sliced garlic

1/4 cup white wine

1/2 cup clam juice

4 cloves Roasted Garlic (page 242)

1/2 teaspoon crushed red pepper flakes

1 dried bay leaf

36 to 40 PEI mussels (substitute a local variety if PEI are not available)

1 1/2 cups canned whole, peeled Italian plum tomatoes

3 tablespoons chopped fresh basil

2 tablespoons chopped fresh flat-leaf parsley

1 teaspoon chopped fresh oregano

1/4 teaspoon kosher salt

Cool-sounding fra diavolo is Italian for "brother devil," but it really translates to one hot and spicy sauce. The sauce is another Italian-American creation that was invented on America's shores, but the culinary logic behind it is purely Old World and makes a delicious and spicy tomato sauce that cuts through the rich flavors of shellfish. The hot spice mix pairs well with a fruit-forward white wine that will calm the spice on your palate—something along the lines of a Gavi, a Falanghina, or a Soave. The dish will still have a good bit of zip that plays wonderfully against the delectable flavor of the mussels. The contrast is enticing and the spice makes for less of a full feeling after eating this main course. Adjust the spiciness up or down to suit your crowd and your own preferences.

*1. Heat the olive oil in a large sauté pan over medium-high heat. Add the garlic and sauté until lightly browned.*

*2. Add the white wine, clam juice, roasted garlic, red pepper flakes, bay leaf, and mussels. As the mussels open, remove them from the pan and set aside; discard any that do not open.*

*3. Add the tomatoes, basil, parsley, oregano, and salt and bring the sauce to a boil. Boil for 4 to 5 minutes, or until the sauce has reduced by one-third, breaking up the tomatoes as they cook.*

*4. Arrange the mussels in a serving bowl and top with the sauce. Serve immediately*

# Cod Puttanesca

*Serves 4 to 6*

3/4 cup olive oil blend (3 parts canola oil to 1 part olive oil)

2 tablespoons all-purpose flour

1/4 teaspoon kosher salt

1/8 teaspoon cracked black pepper

One 22-ounce skinless and boneless cod fillet

2 tablespoons thinly sliced garlic

4 cloves Roasted Garlic (page 242)

1/4 cup halved and thinly sliced red onion

3 tablespoons chopped fresh basil

2 tablespoons chopped fresh flat-leaf parsley

3 tablespoons pitted and halved black Italian olives (Ligurian or Gaeta)

2 cups finely diced fresh Roma tomatoes

2 tablespoons drained capers

1 teaspoon minced anchovies

1/2 cup clam juice

Derived from the Italian word for "a lady of the night," the dish's name is meant to describe common, lowly ingredients. Anchovies supply much of the saline bite, but they are minced and cooked into the sauce, which should satisfy any diner who might have an aversion to this fish. Olives, capers, and tomatoes serve as a savory foundation for a chunky sauce that is an ideal complement to the cod we use in this version.

*1. Heat 6 tablespoons of the oil in a large sauté pan over medium-high heat. In a shallow baking pan, thoroughly mix the flour with the salt and pepper.*

*2. Dredge the cod in the flour mix until both sides are well coated. Shake off any excess. Carefully slide the cod into the pan of hot oil and pan-fry for 2 to 3 minutes on each side, or until nicely browned and just cooked through. Transfer the fish to the paper towel–lined plate and blot off any excess oil. Remove and set aside on a clean plate.*

*3. Add the remaining 6 tablespoons oil to the sauté pan. When the oil is hot, add the sliced garlic and brown lightly. Add the roasted garlic, onion, 1½ tablespoons of the basil and 1 tablespoon of the parsley. Cook until the onions are translucent.*

*4. Add the olives, tomatoes, capers, anchovies, and clam juice and simmer for 5 to 7 minutes (the tomatoes will begin to break down). Add the remaining 1½ tablespoons basil and 1 tablespoon parsley. Taste the sauce, and season with additional salt and pepper if desired.*

*5. Center the fish on a decorative serving platter and top with the sauce. Serve immediately.*

# Broiled Lobster Oreganata

*Serves 4 to 6*

Four 1 to 1¼-pound live lobsters

½ teaspoon kosher salt

¼ teaspoon cracked black pepper

½ cup Garlic Butter (page 248), softened

2 teaspoons chopped fresh oregano

2 cups Carmine's Bread Crumbs (page 244)

2 tablespoons grated Romano cheese

3 tablespoons extra-virgin olive oil

4 cups clam juice

½ pound (2 sticks) unsalted butter

4 teaspoons chopped fresh flat-leaf parsley

3 to 4 lemons, cut into wedges, for garnish

The idea behind any "oreganata" dish is the savory sturdiness of oregano and a dose of breading. In this case, the signature herb blends wonderfully with the opulent sweetness of that richest of shellfish—lobster. The duo calls for a full-bodied white such as Fiano or Chardonnay. The dish requires little beyond some basic ingredients to create an over-the-top sensation that looks wonderful on the plate.

*1. Preheat the oven to 400°F.*

*2. Hold a lobster down on a cutting board; remove the antennas and then flip it so that the underside is facing up. Using a large chef knife, cut lengthwise down the center of the body, from the head to the tail fin. (Don't cut all of the way through; just slice through the shell and into the meat.) With the back of the knife, slightly crack each claw. Repeat with the other lobsters.*

*3. Place the lobsters on a sheet pan (or pans), belly up. Spread each lobster apart, to open along the cut. Season with salt and pepper. Spread the garlic butter generously in the opening from the tail all the way up. Butter the cracked opening in the claws.*

*4. In a small bowl, fold the oregano in with the bread crumbs. Sprinkle the mixture onto the lobster, then top with the Romano cheese and drizzle with the olive oil.*

*5. Pour the clam juice around the lobster on the sheet pan and bake for 18 to 22 minutes, or until the meat is white and firm and the bread crumbs are toasted and browned.*

6. *While the lobsters are cooking, heat the butter in a small pot over low heat. Skim the solids that float to the top, until the butter is entirely clarified. Keep warm.*

7. *Serve the lobsters on a large platter, garnish with the chopped parsley and lemon wedges. Serve with ramekins of the clarified butter.*

# Halibut with Vegetable Risotto

*Serves 4 to 6*

## SEAFOOD

³/₄ cup all-purpose flour

¹/₂ teaspoon kosher salt

¹/₈ teaspoon cracked black pepper

One 24-ounce skinless halibut fillet, cut into 4 equal pieces

¹/₂ pound (10 to 20) dry-packed sea scallops, side muscle removed

³/₄ pound extra-large shrimp, peeled and deveined

³/₄ cup canola oil

## SAUCE

8 tablespoons (1 stick) unsalted butter

2 tablespoons chopped shallots

¹/₄ cup white wine

2 cups clam juice

¹/₄ cup diced fresh plum tomatoes

2 tablespoons chopped fresh basil

2 tablespoons chopped fresh flat-leaf parsley

3 tablespoons fresh lemon juice

¹/₂ teaspoon kosher salt

¹/₈ teaspoon cracked black pepper

1 bunch fresh chives, chopped

Creamy, smooth and succulent, there is little about this dish that is not truly magnificent. The lovely texture of velvety risotto provides the perfect bed for a delicately pan-fried halibut fillet. Shrimps and scallops add even more richness to a dish thick with it, and an exceptional butter sauce finishes the fish with a luxurious deep flavor.

### TO PREPARE THE HALIBUT

*1. In a small bowl, combine the flour, salt, and pepper and mix well. Spread out the mixture on a large plate. Coat the halibut in the flour mixture and dust off any excess. Repeat with the remaining seafood.*

*2. In a large sauté pan over medium heat, heat the canola oil to about 325°F. Gently place the halibut in the pan and brown both sides. Repeat with the scallops and shrimp, working in batches to avoid overcrowding. Transfer the seafood to a sheet pan and set aside. Discard the oil.*

### TO MAKE THE SAUCE

*1. In a medium sauté pan over medium heat, melt 1 tablespoon of the butter for the salt. Add the shallots and sauté for 1 minute, or until translucent.*

*2. Add the wine and cook until the liquid has reduced by half. Add the clam juice, tomatoes, basil, and parsley and cook until the liquid has reduced by a quarter.*

*3. Add the lemon juice, salt, and pepper and simmer for 2 minutes. Stir in the remaining 7 tablespoons butter and the chives.*

## RISOTTO

4 tablespoons ($^1/_2$ stick) unsalted butter

2 tablespoons chopped shallots

$^1/_2$ teaspoon chopped fresh rosemary

$^1/_2$ teaspoon chopped fresh oregano

$^1/_2$ cup julienned sun-dried tomatoes

1 cup quartered crimini mushrooms, cleaned and stems trimmed prior to cutting

$^1/_2$ teaspoon kosher salt

$^1/_8$ teaspoon cracked black pepper

$^1/_4$ cup dry white wine

1 cup medium-grain Italian rice, such as Arborio, Carnaroli, or Vialone Nano

$4^1/_2$ cups clam juice

$^1/_2$ pound medium asparagus, trimmed and cut diagonally into $^1/_2$-inch pieces

*Reduce the heat to low and keep the sauce warm until the risotto is cooked.*

### TO MAKE THE RISOTTO

*1. While the sauce is simmering, make the risotto.*

*2. Heat a 3-quart or larger saucepan over medium-high heat. Add 2 tablespoons of the butter and the shallots and sauté for about 1 minute, or until the shallots are translucent.*

*3. Add the rosemary, oregano, sun-dried tomatoes, mushrooms, salt, and pepper and cook for 2 minutes. Add the wine and cook until the liquid has reduced by half.*

*4. Add the rice and mix until well coated. Add the clam juice, ½ cup at a time, stirring continuously until all the juice has been absorbed, before adding more. Repeat until all but ½ cup of the clam juice has been used.*

*5. Add the asparagus and the remaining ½ cup of clam juice and cook, stirring occasionally, until the asparagus is cooked, the liquid has been absorbed, and the rice is tender. Add the remaining 2 tablespoons butter and stir to incorporate.*

### TO FINISH THE DISH

*1. Preheat the oven to 350°F.*

*2. Reheat the seafood for 3 to 5 minutes in the oven.*

*3. Spread the risotto out on a serving platter, arrange the seafood on top, and spread the sauce evenly over the top.*

# Scallops and Shrimp Scarpariello

*Serves 4 to 6*

3 tablespoons olive oil blend (3 parts canola oil to 1 part olive oil)

4 cloves Roasted Garlic (page 242)

1 tablespoon sliced garlic

1 pound extra-large shrimp, shelled and deveined

1 pound dry-packed jumbo sea scallops, side muscle removed

8 tablespoons plus 1 teaspoon unsalted cold butter, cubed

1 tablespoon chopped shallots

1 tablespoon chopped fresh rosemary

1 tablespoon chopped fresh oregano

1/4 teaspoon crushed red pepper flakes

1/2 cup white wine

1 cup clam juice

2 tablespoons fresh lemon juice

1/4 teaspoon kosher salt

1/8 teaspoon cracked black pepper

Scarpariello is a modest, uncomplicated white wine sauce. You'll find that the flavors in the sauce itself sparkle and provide a splash of acidic bite that counters the overwhelming richness of the shrimp and scallops. The combination makes this dish a pleasure to eat and a meal that will satisfy without being overwhelming.

*1. Heat the oil in a large sauté pan over medium-high heat. Add the garlics and the shrimp and quickly sauté until the shrimp are just slightly browned on both sides. Remove the shrimp and set aside. Repeat the process with the scallops.*

*2. Pour off the excess oil, keeping the garlic in the pan. Add 1 teaspoon of the butter and the shallots and sauté until the shallots are translucent.*

*3. Add the rosemary, oregano, red pepper flakes, and white wine and cook until the liquid has reduced by half.*

*4. Add the clam juice and cook until the liquid has again reduced by half. Gradually whisk in the remaining 8 tablespoons butter, allowing each piece to melt before adding the next. When all the butter is incorporated, add the lemon juice, salt, and pepper.*

*5. Return the shellfish to the pan and adjust the heat to maintain a light simmer. Cook until the shellfish is cooked through, 1 to 2 minutes. Serve on a large serving platter.*

# Meat and Chicken

In the tough economic circumstances leading up to the massive migration to America, it was the rare Southern Italian household that could afford to regularly serve chicken, much less beef. These culinary luxuries became the stuff of special-occasion meals in the cuisine that immigrants brought with them to American shores. They continued to be cause for celebration at the Sunday dinners in grandma's backyard. The richness of a properly cooked Osso Buco (page 163) or carefully simmered Chicken Cacciatore (page 148) were the highest expressions of what meat and chicken could be on a dinner plate.

Carmine's chefs consider chicken a canvas on which flavors are painted. Slowly simmered, or breaded and quickly fried, chicken absorbs the flavors with which it comes in contact. Traditional Italian components such as olive oil and tomato sauce are ideal for keeping chicken moist and tender, and a few simple spices are all that's needed to make chicken really sing in an Italian recipe.

Meat presents a greater variety of options, from the pleasant mild sweetness of lamb, to the hearty flavor of beef. It can be the star of the show, as it is in our Porterhouse Pizzaiola (page 161) or more of a bit player, such as in our Beef Involtini (page 177). We take great care to match the meat in our recipes to the cooking style most appropriate for the cut. Slowly simmered sauces are just the thing to break down tough but flavorful cuts into fork-tender perfection. A quick sear, on the other hand, may be all that's required for a naturally tender piece of meat that is to be coupled with a simple light ragu featuring tomatoes, garlic, and wine.

Whether you're cooking chicken or meat, success begins with the shopping. The freshest meat and poultry will always be the healthiest and tastiest. A local butcher is a wonderful way to go, and will lavish more care on the cuts than the person stocking a supermarket meat case might. Always look for labels that include the words "vegetarian fed," "grass fed," "free range," or—the best—"USDA Organic." These cuts will cost a little more, but the difference in flavor will be noticeable, and you'll be doing your family and friends a favor by feeding them as healthily as possible.

# Chicken Cacciatore

*Serves 4 to 6*

## CHICKEN

1 pound all-purpose flour

1 teaspoon kosher salt

1/4 teaspoon cracked black pepper

1 1/2 cups canola oil

Two 3-pound whole chickens, cut into 10 pieces each

## SAUCE

1/2 cup Garlic Oil (page 242)

1 1/2 cups diced white onions

1 cup diced red bell peppers

1 cup diced green bell peppers

1/3 cup sliced garlic

2 dried bay leaves

2 tablespoons chopped fresh flat-leaf parsley

2 tablespoons chopped fresh oregano leaves

2 tablespoons chopped fresh basil

1 tablespoon fresh rosemary

1 pound crimini mushrooms, cleaned, stems trimmed, mushrooms quartered

1 1/2 teaspoons kosher salt

1/4 teaspoon cracked black pepper

1 cup white wine

*Cacciatore* translates to "hunter," but the title really refers to the rustic preparation style used by a woodsman hunter at the end of day. We serve ours over rich egg noodles, although you can substitute your favorite pasta. Beyond that, the full-bodied sauce needs little in the way of accompaniment, just a loaf of your favorite crusty country bread and perhaps a nice glass of Montepulciano d'Abruzzo.

### TO PREPARE THE CHICKEN

*1. Preheat the oven to 350°F. Line a sheet pan with paper towels.*

*2. In a medium bowl, whisk together the flour, salt, and black pepper. Heat the canola oil in a large sauté pan over medium-high heat.*

*3. Dredge each piece of chicken in the seasoned flour and shake off any excess.*

*4. Working in batches to avoid overcrowding, carefully place the floured chicken in the skillet and fry until nicely browned. Flip each piece and brown the opposite side. Transfer the seared chicken to the lined sheet pan.*

### TO MAKE THE SAUCE

*1. In a separate large pan over high heat, combine the garlic oil, onions, and bell peppers. Sauté until the vegetables begin to brown, then add the garlic and cook for 1 to 2 minutes.*

*2. Add the bay leaves, parsley, oregano, basil, rosemary, and mushrooms and cook for 5 minutes. Add the salt, black pepper,*

4 cups canned whole, peeled Italian plum tomatoes

1 cup chicken stock

1 cup Brown Sauce (page 249)

12 ounces wide egg noodles, cooked al dente

and white wine and cook for 2 to 3 minutes. Add the tomatoes, chicken stock, and brown sauce and bring to a boil. Cook until the liquid is reduced by one-quarter.

TO FINISH THE DISH

1. In a 4-quart casserole dish, combine the chicken and the sauce. Cover and bake for 35 minutes.

2. When the chicken has almost finished cooking, cook the egg noodles. Spread the cooked pasta in the center of a large serving platter. Arrange the chicken pieces over the noodles, top with the sauce, and serve.

# Chicken Cutlet

*Serves 4 to 6*

1 cup all-purpose flour

$1/2$ teaspoon kosher salt

$1/8$ teaspoon cracked black pepper

6 extra-large eggs, beaten

5 cups Carmine's Bread Crumbs (page 244)

$1\frac{1}{2}$ cups canola oil

$1\frac{1}{2}$ pounds boneless, skinless chicken breasts, pounded out to thickness of $3/8$ inch

3 to 4 lemons, cut into wedges, for garnish

The perfect chicken cutlet is all about the crunch. The lightly seasoned coating in the Carmine's version not only adds a nice bit of spice to the chicken, it helps keep the juices inside. A simple breaded chicken cutlet eaten with nothing more than a spritz of fresh lemon juice is an absolute delight. Of course, this favorite also lends itself to embellishment if you prefer—you can even cover the cutlet with marinara sauce and mozzarella, and bake it for a lovely *parmigiana*.

*1. In a shallow pan, whisk together the flour, salt, and pepper. Add the eggs to a separate shallow pan. Fill a third pan with the bread crumbs. Line a sheet pan with several layers of paper towels.*

*2. Heat the oil in a large sauté pan over medium-high heat until the oil reaches 325°F.*

*3. Dredge 1 to 2 pieces of the chicken in the flour, coating both sides. Shake off any excess. Dip the floured pieces into the eggs, and let any excess drip off. Press the pieces into the bread crumbs until the chicken pieces are entirely coated. Knock off the excess crumbs.*

*4. Slide the chicken into the hot oil and fry for 2 to 3 minutes per side, until nicely browned all over and thoroughly cooked. Transfer the fried cutlets to the lined sheet pan to cool. Pat the tops dry with paper towels. Repeat until all the cutlets are fried.*

*5. Serve the cutlets on a platter garnished with lemon wedges and accompany with a bowl of Carmine's Marinara Sauce (page 251) on the side, if desired.*

# Chicken Francese

*Serves 4 to 6*

## CHICKEN

1 cup all-purpose flour

1¹/₂ teaspoons kosher salt

³/₈ teaspoon cracked black pepper

3 extra-large eggs, beaten

5 tablespoons chopped fresh
   flat-leaf parsley

³/₄ cup canola oil

1 pound boneless, skinless chicken
   breast, cut scallopine (page 153)

## SAUCE

8 tablespoons (1 stick) unsalted
   butter

1 tablespoon chopped shallots

¹/₂ cup white wine

2 cups chicken stock

1 teaspoon salt

¹/₄ teaspoon cracked black pepper

2 tablespoons fresh lemon juice

## SPINACH

¹/₄ cup olive oil

1 tablespoon sliced garlic

1 pound spinach leaves, well rinsed,
   dried, ends trimmed

As you might have guessed by the name, this Italian-American dish (developed in New York City) appropriates a delicate French lemon sauce as the ideal coating for chicken cutlets. The coating ensures a heavenly crunch that goes right along with the pleasingly light sauce. The dish is elegant on the table, with the perfect look and lightness for a single course in a dinner party.

### TO PREPARE THE CHICKEN

*1. In a shallow pan, whisk together the flour, ½ teaspoon of the salt, and ¹/₈ teaspoon of the pepper. Add the eggs and 2 tablespoons of the chopped parsley to a separate shallow pan. Line a sheet pan with several layers of paper towels.*

*2. Heat the canola oil in a large sauté pan over medium-high heat until the oil reaches 325°F.*

*3. Dredge 2 to 3 pieces of the chicken in the flour, coating both sides. Shake off any excess. Hold the chicken with tongs and dunk it in the eggs, letting any excess drip off.*

*4. Slide the chicken into the oil and fry very briefly, just until lightly browned. Transfer the chicken to the paper towel–lined sheet pan. Repeat with the remaining chicken.*

### TO MAKE THE SAUCE

*1. In a large sauté pan over medium-high heat, melt 1 tablespoon of the butter. Add the shallots and sauté until translucent. Add the white wine and cook until the liquid has reduced by half.*

*2. Add the chicken stock and salt and pepper and cook until the liquid has again reduced by half. Set aside.*

TO PREPARE THE SPINACH

*Heat the olive oil in a separate sauté pan over medium-high heat. Add the garlic and sauté until nicely browned. Add the spinach and sauté it very quickly, just until the spinach starts wilting. Remove the spinach and blot as much of the moisture from the leaves as possible with paper towels. Set aside.*

TO FINISH THE DISH

*1. Return the sauce to a boil and add the lemon juice. Reduce the heat to a simmer, and whisk in the remaining 7 tablespoons butter. Add the chicken to the sauce, and cook just until it is warmed through.*

*2. Spread the spinach out in the center of a serving platter. Top with the chicken, and then pour the sauce over both. Garnish with the remaining 3 tablespoons chopped parsley and serve.*

## ———— CARMINE'S KITCHEN WISDOM ————

Cutting "scallopine" is a basic Italian kitchen skill. Buy small whole boneless, skinless chicken breasts, separate the lobes, and butterfly the breasts, working from the thick end to the thin, with a very sharp, thin boning knife. Pound the breasts out between two pieces of plastic wrap until they are about ¼-inch thick.

# Chicken Sorrentino

*Serves 4 to 6*

## CHEESE MIXTURE

2 cups whole-milk ricotta cheese

$1/4$ cup shredded whole-milk mozzarella cheese

4 tablespoons grated Romano cheese

1 tablespoon chopped fresh flat-leaf parsley

$1/4$ teaspoon kosher salt

$1/8$ teaspoon cracked black pepper

$1/2$ teaspoon dried oregano leaves

## CUTLETS

$1^1/2$ cups all-purpose flour

$1/4$ teaspoon kosher salt

$1/4$ teaspoon cracked black pepper

5 extra-large eggs (beat 3 in one portion, and 2 in another)

$2^1/4$ cups canola oil

$1/2$ pound eggplant, ends cut off and sliced lengthwise, $3/8$-inch thick

4 tablespoons chopped fresh flat-leaf parsley

5 tablespoons grated Romano cheese

1 pound boneless, skinless chicken breasts, cut into thin scallopine (see page 153)

It's hard to go wrong when you start out with breaded eggplant and chicken cutlets, an irresistible combination of delicately crunchy exteriors around mildly savory, tender, and moist interiors. That combo is the sturdy base for this dish, dressed in an over-the-top melted cheese blend comprised of three uniquely different Italian cheeses. Bake it just right so that all the flavors meld into a shamelessly decadent meal.

### TO PREPARE THE CHEESE MIXTURE

*In a medium bowl, combine all the ingredients for the cheese mixture. Mix thoroughly, cover, and refrigerate.*

### TO PREPARE THE CUTLETS AND EGGPLANT

*1. In a shallow pan, whisk together the flour, salt, and pepper for the cutlets. Add 3 beaten eggs to a separate shallow pan. Line a sheet pan with several layers of paper towels.*

*2. Heat the canola oil in a large sauté pan over medium-high heat until the oil reaches 325°F.*

*3. Dip a slice of eggplant in the flour, coating both sides. Shake off any excess. Using tongs, dip the eggplant into the beaten eggs. Let any excess drip off. Slide the eggplant into the hot oil. Repeat with another slice of eggplant. Work like this in batches of 2 to 3 slices, to avoid overcrowding the pan. Fry until the slices are nicely browned on all sides, 1 to 2 minutes per side. Transfer the fried slices to the lined sheet pan and pat the top of each slice dry with more paper towels.*

3 cups Carmine's Bread Crumbs
(page 244)

1/2 cup fresh basil leaves

1/4 pound prosciutto, thinly sliced

1/2 pound whole-milk mozzarella
cheese, thinly sliced

4 cups Carmine's Marinara Sauce
(page 251), heated

*4. Add the remaining 2 eggs to the leftover beaten eggs with 2 tablespoons of chopped parsley and 3 tablespoons of the Romano cheese and mix well. Add the bread crumbs to a third shallow pan.*

*5. Dredge a chicken cutlet in the flour and shake off any excess. Dip it into the egg mixture, allowing any extra to drip off. Firmly press it into the bread crumbs, to ensure it is coated all around. Knock off any excess crumbs.*

*6. Working in batches to avoid overcrowding, carefully slide the chicken into the oil and fry for 1 to 2 minutes per side, or until nicely browned on both sides. Transfer the chicken to the lined sheet pan and blot with paper towels to remove excess oil. Repeat until all the chicken cutlets are fried.*

TO ASSEMBLE AND FINISH THE DISH

*1. Preheat the oven to 350°F.*

*2. Spread the chicken cutlets out on a nonstick sheet pan. Place a piece of eggplant on top of each cutlet, cutting the sides of the eggplant as necessary to ensure it perfectly covers the cutlet. Spread about 2 tablespoons of the cheese mixture on top of each eggplant, covering the eggplant.*

*3. Layer basil leaves on top of the cheese mixture. Cover with a slice of prosciutto followed finally by a slice of mozzarella; be sure to cover the entire surface with one ingredient prior to adding the next.*

*4. Bake for 10 to 15 minutes, or until the cheese has melted and is beginning to brown. Ladle the marinara sauce onto a large oval serving platter. Shingle the chicken on top and garnish with the remaining 2 tablespoons Romano cheese and 2 tablespoons parsley.*

A beautiful simplicity lies at the heart of all great Italian cooking. The magic involves a limited number of high-quality ingredients held together by just the right spices and herbs. Balance is crucial, because even in small amounts a spice or herb can radically affect a recipe. That's why we never use a dried herb where fresh was intended, or vice versa. Dried herbs have a more intense flavor than the fresh version, although fresh usually feature a purer, more characteristic flavor. The flavor of dried herbs will fade over time. Store them in a cool, dry, dark place to keep them at their best. The outside limits for optimum flavor is one year for cut herbs (like oregano), three years for ground herbs such as nutmeg, and five years for whole spices such as peppercorns.

## SPICES

**Kosher salt:** Larger grains and a lighter flavor mark this seasoning. But be careful in drier recipes, because this salt needs significant moisture to fully dissolve.

**Black pepper:** Grind or crack your pepper fresh. A pepper mill is a must in the kitchen: simply loosen to crack the pepper and tighten to grind. Try colored peppercorns for slightly different flavors and a splash of color.

**Dried oregano:** Italian cooking uses Mediterranean oregano, with a subtler flavor than the Mexican variety. However, oregano is still a fairly pungent spice and should always be used in moderation.

**Dried basil:** The dried form is noticeably less rich and well-rounded than fresh basil. It is usually used alone or coupled with a limited number of other herbs, such as oregano.

**Fennel seed:** This spice boasts an anise aroma and flavor, and a little goes a long way.

**Bay leaf:** Fresh bay leaves are used for their strong aroma and slight bitterness, and they are most often removed after the dish is cooked because the sharp edges of the leaves present a modest risk to the digestive tract and airway. The dried version is used regularly in Italian recipes, for its herbal and floral tones. It blends well with other typically Italian herbs, such as oregano.

**Thyme:** Both fresh and dried versions of this Mediterranean herb are used in Italian cooking. The fresh version is noticeably more well-rounded, featuring hints of mint and lemon. The dried version is more powerful, and a common addition to soups, stews, and heavy sauces.

**Pepperoncino chili flakes:** Also called crushed red pepper flakes, these are made from the Italian pepperoncino pepper, dried and cut into flakes. They can be used to add just a little heat; the flakes are mildly hot, so they won't overpower the other ingredients in the dish.

**Saffron:** Harvested from the domesticated crocus flower, saffron is used sparingly in Italian cooking. But when it's called for, there is no substitute. It is only sold dried, and the flavor is complex, with notes of honey and hay. It is also a powerful orangish-yellow coloring agent.

**Garlic powder:** This is garlic cloves that have been dried and finely powdered. The flavor is not as strong or complex as fresh garlic, but it's great for giving sauces, marinades, or soups a slight essence of the herb.

**Onion powder:** Made from dehydrated and ground onions, onion powder is less pungent and sweeter. It is a way to add onion flavor to soups, stews, sauces, and marinades easily and quickly.

**Coriander:** This Italian cooking favorite is used as an herb, and in two forms as a spice. Also called cilantro, fresh coriander leaves are added to soups and used as garnish to add a citrus tone. Coriander seeds and ground coriander are used in soups and sauces.

**Ginger:** This spice is used sparingly because it has a sharp, distinctive, and slightly hot flavor that can overwhelm other notes in a dish.

**Nutmeg:** The spice can be ground fresh or used dried (we prefer the fresh version, because the difference is noticeable).

## HERBS

**Fresh Rosemary:** The rich smell and pleasantly bitter, somewhat piney taste of rosemary is magic on meat and in sauces.

**Fresh Basil:** Delicate, slightly sweet and with an earthy smell, basil is ideal for salads, pastas, and other creamy cheeses. The herb loses flavor quickly when cooked, which is why it is most often used fresh and sliced as a garnish.

**Flat-leaf Parsley:** Sometimes labeled Italian parsley, this version has a slightly stronger flavor than the more ubiquitous curly parsley, but the earthy, grassy tones are still subdued enough that this is used as an accent herb in most dishes.

**Sage:** Sage's strong savory flavor has an earthy appeal that pairs perfectly with any meat, and makes for a complex mix when combined with other strong herbs such as oregano.

**Marjoram:** Marjoram comes from the same species of plant as oregano, but marjoram has a mellower, aromatic floral nature, with less bite than oregano. Fresh leaves will keep refrigerated for about a week. Crushed, dried leaves will remain usable for about a year.

# Chicken Marsala

*Serves 2 to 4*

1 cup all-purpose flour

Kosher salt

Freshly ground black pepper

Six to seven 1½-ounce chicken cutlets (or substitute veal cutlets if desired)

½ cup olive oil blend (3 parts canola oil to 1 part olive oil)

2 tablespoons unsalted butter

1 large shallot, finely chopped

2 cups sliced crimini mushrooms, cleaned, stem ends trimmed prior to slicing

½ cup Marsala wine

1 cup Brown Sauce (page 249)

This is a wonderful cold-weather meal, and should be served with crusty country bread to sop up the amazing sauce. It's especially good when served with a fruit-forward, medium-bodied red wine like Negro Amaro or Amarone.

*1. Spread the flour on a large plate and season it with salt and pepper. Coat both sides of the chicken with flour and shake off any excess.*

*2. Heat the oil in a large sauté pan over medium-high heat. When the oil is hot, add the cutlets, one at a time, and cook for about 2 minutes per side, or until the cutlet is lightly browned all over. Transfer to a plate. Repeat to cook the remaining cutlets.*

*3. Discard the oil from the pan. Reduce the heat to medium and add 1 tablespoon of the butter. When it has melted, add the shallots and cook, stirring, for about 2 minutes, or until they are lightly browned and softened.*

*4. Add the mushrooms to the pan, increase the heat to high, and cook for 2 minutes stirring as little as possible. Remove the pan from the heat and add the wine. Return the pan to the heat and cook the sauce for about 1 minute, or until bubbling. The wine may flame, but will die out after a minute or so.*

*5. Add the Brown Sauce, reduce the heat to medium, and let the sauce simmer for 2 to 3 minutes. Add the remaining 1 table-spoon of butter and stir it in. Season with salt and pepper.*

*6. Return the cutlets to the pan of sauce to warm through and absorb some of the sauce's flavor. Transfer the cutlets to a platter, ladle the sauce over them, and serve.*

# Chicken Saltimbocca

*Serves 2 to 4*

Six 2-ounce chicken cutlets (or substitute veal cutlets as desired)

2 tablespoons unsalted butter

6 fresh sage leaves

3 thin slices prosciutto, cut in half crosswise

1 cup all-purpose flour

Kosher salt

Freshly ground black pepper

$^1/_2$ cup olive oil blend (3 parts canola oil to 1 part olive oil)

1 tablespoon chopped shallots

$^1/_4$ cup dry white wine

1 cup Brown Sauce (page 249)

$^1/_4$ cup olive oil

2 tablespoons coarsely chopped garlic

2 pounds fresh spinach, well rinsed, stems removed

6 thin slices fresh mozzarella cheese (about 1$^1/_2$ ounces)

This dish is a tumble of savory flavors that does justice to the translation of saltimbocca, "jump into the mouth." We make ours with white wine rather than Marsala, so it's a little zestier. We also use chicken, but you can substitute veal cutlets for a slightly sweeter, meatier appeal.

*1. Cover a work surface with plastic wrap. Lay the cutlets out on the plastic wrap. Put ½ teaspoon of butter on top of each cutlet, then 1 sage leaf, and top with a slice of prosciutto. Place another sheet of plastic wrap over the cutlets and, using a mallet or small, heavy frying pan, lightly pound the prosciutto until it adheres to the meat and the cutlets flatten slightly. Remove the plastic wrap and discard it.*

*2. Spread the flour on a large plate and season lightly with salt and pepper. Coat the cutlets with flour and shake off any excess.*

*3. Heat the oil in a large sauté pan over medium-high heat. When the oil is hot, add the cutlets, prosciutto-side down, and cook for about 2 minutes, or until they are lightly browned. Flip the cutlets and repeat. Transfer to a plate and set aside.*

*4. Discard any oil from the pan. Reduce the heat to medium and add 1 tablespoon of the butter. When it has melted, add the shallots and cook them, stirring, for about 2 minutes, or until they are browned and softened.*

*5. Add the wine and cook the shallots for about 30 seconds. Add the Brown Sauce and bring to a simmer. Add the cutlets and*

*(continued)*

simmer them for about 3 minutes. Adjust the heat to maintain a simmer.

6. Heat the olive oil in a separate sauté pan over medium-high heat. Add the garlic and sauté until nicely browned. Add the spinach and sauté it very quickly, just until the spinach starts wilting. Remove the spinach and blot as much of the moisture from the leaves as possible with a paper towel. Set aside.

7. Preheat the broiler.

8. Remove the cutlets from the sauce and transfer them to a shallow ovenproof casserole that will fit under the broiler. Place a slice of mozzarella on top of each cutlet. Broil the cutlets for 30 seconds to 1 minute, or until the cheese has melted.

9. Spread the spinach down the center of a large platter. Put the chicken on top of the spinach. Pour the sauce over the top and serve.

# Porterhouse Pizzaiola

*Serves 4 to 6*

## STEAK

One 45-ounce Porterhouse steak

3 teaspoons kosher salt

1/2 teaspoon cracked black pepper

2 tablespoons dried oregano

1 1/2 tablespoons garlic powder

2 tablespoons olive oil

2 tablespoons Garlic-Herb Oil (page 243), for drizzling

## SAUCE

1/4 cup olive oil

1/2 pound red bell peppers, cored, seeded, and diced large

1/2 pound green bell peppers, cored, seeded, and diced large

1 pound white onions, diced large

1/4 cup sliced garlic

3/4 teaspoon kosher salt

1/8 teaspoon cracked black pepper

1/2 cup white wine

1 cup canned whole, peeled Italian plum tomatoes with purée

1 tablespoon chopped fresh flat-leaf parsley

1 teaspoon chopped fresh oregano

4 tablespoons chopped fresh basil

There is something uniquely satisfying about a high-quality steak. It only becomes more satisfying with the sauce and toppings that are more commonly found on a delicious pizza. It's not like it needs much amplification, though; a Porterhouse is essentially a T-bone steak, full of fine marbling and perfect flavor.

### TO PREPARE THE STEAK

*1. Preheat the broiler or grill on medium.*

*2. Season the steak on both sides with the salt and pepper, then with the oregano and garlic powder. Drizzle each side with olive oil.*

*3. Broil or grill until the steak reaches the appropriate temperature for the doneness that you prefer (see chart on page 162).*

### TO MAKE THE SAUCE

*1. While the steak is cooking, heat the olive oil in a large sauté pan over medium-high heat. When the oil is hot, add the bell peppers and onions and cook until they begin to brown.*

*2. Add the garlic, salt, and black pepper and cook until the mixture is nicely browned, 3 to 5 minutes. Add the white wine and cook for 2 to 3 minutes more.*

*3. Add the tomatoes, parsley, oregano, basil, red pepper flakes, and marinara sauce and cook until the sauce reduces slightly and begins to thicken.*

*(continued)*

¼ teaspoon crushed red pepper
flakes

1 cup Carmine's Marinara Sauce
(page 251)

### TO FINISH THE DISH

*1. Remove the steak from the oven or grill and set aside to rest for 5 minutes.*

*2. Using a thin, narrow boning knife, cut each side (the strip and the filet) off the bone. Set the bone aside. Cut each side separately, slicing the meat against the grain into ¼-inch slices. Keep the slices together as you cut.*

*3. Ladle the sauce onto a large platter, and spread the ingredients evenly across the surface. Place the bone in the center of the platter, and reconstruct the sliced filet, but shingle the sliced steak. Drizzle the garlic-herb oil over the steak and serve.*

---

## CARMINE'S KITCHEN WISDOM

A meat thermometer is a must-have in any kitchen. You can buy an inexpensive basic unit or a more high-tech option that will set you back a pretty penny, but all work well. You'll hear about a lot of homespun ways to determine doneness, like feeling parts of your hand and comparing that to how the steak feels, but there simply is no substitute for a proper meat thermometer. The list below shows the most recently updated USDA recommendations for doneness by temperature. Keep in mind that the USDA always errs on the side of safety (for instance, there is no USDA recommendation for rare, because they don't recommend serving steak rare). Most pros use lower temperatures, similar to what we've listed here.

### BEEF STEAK

**Rare:** (USDA) n/r (Recom.) 120°F
**Medium Rare:** (USDA) 145°F (Recom.) 125–130°F
**Medium:** (USDA) 160°F (Recom.) 140–145°F
**Medium Well:** (USDA) 160°F (Recom.) 145–150°F
**Well:** (USDA) 170°F (Recom.) 155°F or more

### PORK

**Medium Rare:** (USDA) n/r (Recom.) 145°F
**Medium:** (USDA) 160°F (Recom.) 150°F
**Well:** (USDA) 170°F (Recom.) 160°F

# Osso Buco

*Serves 4 to 6*

1¹/₄ cups olive oil blend (3 parts canola oil to 1 part olive oil)

1¹/₂ cups all-purpose flour

1 tablespoon kosher salt

1 teaspoon cracked black pepper

8 pounds veal hind shank, crosscut into 2¹/₂-inch sections

1¹/₂ cups finely diced celery

1¹/₂ cups finely diced carrots

1¹/₂ cups finely diced white onions

¹/₄ cup sliced garlic

2 cups red wine

Zest of 2 lemons

Zest of 2 oranges

1 tablespoon chopped fresh flat-leaf parsley

1 teaspoon chopped fresh rosemary

1 tablespoon chopped fresh basil

1 tablespoon chopped fresh oregano

6 cups Brown Sauce (page 249)

6 cups chicken stock

1 cup tomato paste

We have the chefs of Milan to thank for this spectacular veal dish that redefines how tender meat can be. The red wine sauce that graces the meat is a luscious coating that is brightened with the lightest touch of citrus. We serve it with saffron risotto, but you can serve it plain as described here.

*1. Heat the oil in a large (at least 8-quart), low-profile pot over medium-high heat. In a medium bowl, mix the flour, 1 teaspoon of the salt, and ¼ teaspoon of the pepper. Line a plate with paper towels.*

*2. Dredge the veal pieces in the flour mixture and shake off the excess. Working in batches to avoid overcrowding, carefully place the veal pieces in the hot oil and cook until all sides are nicely browned. Transfer the veal to the paper towel–lined plate and set aside. Pour off about half of the oil remaining in the pot.*

*3. Add the celery, carrots, and onions to the pot. When they begin to brown, add the garlic and sauté for 2 minutes. Add the wine and remaining 2 teaspoons salt and ¼ teaspoon pepper and cook until the liquid has reduced by half.*

*4. Add the remaining ingredients, except for the veal, and bring to a boil. Boil for 5 minutes.*

*5. Gently return the veal shank to the pot and reduce the heat to a simmer. Cover and cook for 2 to 2½ hours, or until the veal is fork-tender, but not falling off the bone.*

*6. Using tongs, transfer the veal shanks to a deep serving platter. Pour the sauce over the top and serve.*

# Sausage, Peppers, Potatoes, and Onions

*Serves 4 to 6*

1½ pounds russet potatoes

1 teaspoon kosher salt

¼ teaspoon cracked black pepper

½ teaspoon dried oregano

1 cup olive oil

1½ pounds link sweet Italian sausage

¾ pound red bell peppers, cored, seeded, and diced large

¾ pound green bell peppers, cored, seeded, and diced large

1 pound white onions, peeled and diced large

⅓ cup sliced garlic

3 tablespoons chopped fresh flat-leaf parsley

1 tablespoon chopped fresh oregano

3 tablespoons chopped fresh basil

¼ teaspoon crushed red pepper flakes

1 teaspoon chopped fresh oregano

4 tablespoons chopped fresh basil

Some Italian recipes are all about re-creating fond memories of family dinners—or ideal for creating new ones. This is just that type of dish, comforting in every way possible. Peppers, potatoes, and onions go together as naturally as an old married couple, and sweet Italian sausage is a savory taste delight that makes every other sausage pale in comparison.

1. *Preheat the oven to 350°F.*

2. *Wash and cut the potatoes crosswise into ³/₈-inch-thick slices. Combine the potatoes in a medium bowl with ½ teaspoon of the salt and ¼ teaspoon of the black pepper, the dried oregano, and ½ cup of the oil. Toss to coat.*

3. *On a nonstick sheet pan, spread the potato slices out in one layer and bake for 20 to 25 minutes. Flip each slice and bake for 10 minutes more, or until browned.*

4. *Spread the sausage on a separate sheet pan and bake for about 20 minutes, turning occasionally, until cooked through and nicely browned. Remove the potatoes and sausages from the oven and set aside to cool.*

5. *Heat the remaining ½ cup olive oil in a large sauté pan over medium-high heat. Add the bell peppers and onions and sauté until they begin to brown. Add the garlic, and the remaining ½ teaspoon salt and ¼ teaspoon black pepper and cook until the mixture is nicely browned.*

6. *Add the parsley, oregano, basil, red pepper flakes, and potatoes and sauté until heated through.*

7. *Add the sausage (cut larger links into diagnal slices) to the pan and toss to coat. Cook until the sausage is heated through, then transfer the mixture to a serving platter and serve.*

As recently as the early twentieth century, pigs roamed free in much of the Italian countryside, rounded up only when it came time for slaughter. Their diet, including such distinctive additions as acorns and mushrooms (as well as many less savory ingredients), ensured that the pork products that came from the pig were full of unique and delicious flavors. Pigs in the wild were such good food hunters that they were even used to unearth underground treasure troves of truffles, until the practice was banned in Italy in the 1980s; the pigs' hooves were introducing disease that was decimating colonies of the precious fungus.

Although they no longer roam free, many Italian pigs—particularly the black-and-white Cinta Senese breed raised in Tuscany—are still fed a largely natural diet and allowed ample space to roam. Traditional Italian methods of raising pigs translate to a fatter animal than the industrial raised pigs of America. Italian pigs will often also have deeper, richer flavors—which come through in the pork products made from those pigs.

The added flavor is apparent in all cuts of the animal. However, even though Italian cooking includes some spectacular pork chop and pork loin recipes, and creative uses for cuts like the pork cheek and pork belly, Italy's best-known pork products are cured ham, bacon, and distinctive sausages. Each of these can be used in so many dishes, and in so many ways, that what we know as Italian cooking would be inconceivable without them.

Prosciutto is not only one of the most treasured pork products of Italy, it is one of the most treasured of all Italian ingredients. Perfectly cured and sliced paper thin, prosciutto is a delicate, savory delicacy ready to eat as soon as it is sliced. It is ideal on sandwiches, from the hot panini to the cold hero. It is often wrapped around melon, vegetables, or hard cheese to make a simple, quick-to-prepare, and refreshing antipasto. It can even be added to pasta or salads after being quickly crisped in a hot skillet.

Regardless of how you hope to use this delicious gift of the pig, you must buy quality to taste quality. There are many domestic prosciuttos that simply can't compare to a high-quality Prosciutto di Parma or Prosciutto San Daniele. These have long been the gold standard of imported prosciuttos, and the package should include the full name and a stamp announcing the contents as "A Product of Italy." The difference in flavor is well worth the difference in cost. If you can find a high-end butcher who will cut fresh prosciutto from an imported ham, you've found a treasure worth holding dear.

Recently, some companies have begun importing a premier and superior prosciutto from Tuscany, Prosciutto Toscano. The difference in this prosciutto lies in the curing process. Where most other prosciuttos are cured just in salt, Prosciutto Toscano is cured in a mixture of salt and traditional spices, which gives the pork a somewhat more robust, and a certainly more complex, flavor. If you can find this version, it's well worth the extra money. You'll know an authentic package of Prosciutto Toscano because, like high-quality Italian olive oils and balsamic vinegars, it will be labeled "DOP" for "Denominazione d'Origine Protetta"—meaning the ham has been grown, cured, and packaged in the designated geographic region using tightly regulated processes.

**Pancetta** is considered the Italian equivalent of bacon, but there are a few key differences. Pancetta, like bacon, is cured pork belly. But unlike its American equivalent, pancetta is not smoked. Consequently, it has a lighter, more purely pork flavor, tinged with a kiss of the spices used in the curing process.

Another difference is the form in which pancetta is sold. You can find it as flat slabs (called *stesa*) or as thin slices from a roll (*arrotolata*). Flat pancetta is sliced or cubed for use in stews, with sautéed greens, and added to pasta sauces. The thinner slices from rolls can be quick fried for crumbling over salads or on top of soups, or served raw as an antipasto, much as prosciutto would be used. You can also find packages of cubed pancetta that will save you prepping the ingredient for recipes. Pancetta is an excellent substitute for any classic Italian recipe that calls for the Italian cured pork cheek *guanciale*.

Like bacon, pancetta in the package should appear uniformly pink, and the abundant fat should be a creamy white, not yellow.

**Capicola** is dry-cured pork shoulder or neck, sliced very thin. Italian-Americans famously refer to it by the slang *gabagoul*, and it is also sold under the name coppa. Whatever you call it, it is one of the most distinctive Italian pork products. It is cured with a vivid mix of strong spices, usually including garlic, and sometimes even red wine. After curing, it is salted, aged, and often smoked—being flavored further by the choice of wood used in the smoking

process. The spices and preparation give capicola a flavor closer to salami than to prosciutto, and this delectable offering makes an assertive addition to a meat-and-cheese antipasti platter. It also adds abundant, unmistakable flavors to any Italian sandwich. A few slices are even wonderful all by themselves as a quick snack.

**Italian sausages** of all kinds can be either culinary bit players or superstars in their own right. Traditionally, the sausage has been flavored noticeably with anise or fennel seed and is offered mild or hot, with the addition of crushed red pepper flakes (which can somewhat mask the fennel overtones).

Grilling the sausages is a tradition in many Italian-American homes, and grilled sausages can be used to make sandwiches or eaten hot off the grill. Italian sausages can also be broken up and used in soups, stews, side dishes, pasta sauces, and stuffings. The sausages can be sliced and then pan-fried and placed on slices of Italian bread with a drizzle of olive oil, to create an incredibly simple and wonderfully satisfying antipasto. Of course, left whole, the sausage is the centerpiece of traditional sausage and peppers. Italian sausage is also a perfect partner to greens from broccoli rabe to chard.

# Rack of Lamb

*Serves 4 to 6*

**SAUCE (yields about 2½ cups)**

¼ cup olive oil blend (3 parts canola oil to 1 part olive oil)

2 pounds lamb neck bones, cut into 2-inch pieces

1 cup finely diced celery

1 cup finely diced carrots

1 cup finely diced white onion

1 teaspoon kosher salt

¼ teaspoon cracked black pepper

¼ cup red wine

6 cups Brown Sauce (page 249)

½ cup chicken stock

1½ tablespoons thinly sliced garlic

2 tablespoons chopped shallots

1 teaspoon whole black peppercorns

¼ cup green Cerignola olives, pitted and chopped

¼ cup black Ligurian olives, pitted and chopped

¼ cup julienned sun-dried tomatoes

1 tablespoon unsalted butter

**LAMB**

1 teaspoon dried oregano

1 teaspoon garlic powder

2 teaspoons kosher salt

½ teaspoon cracked black pepper

Rack of lamb is the classic Italian Easter dinner. It is a filling, all-in-one main course, and we serve it with spectacular Crusty Rosemary Potatoes (page 201) and Roasted Vegetables (page 202) to accompany the delicately sweet meat. Add a bottle of rich red wine like Amarone or Nero d'Avola, and your guests will remember the meal for a long time.

**TO MAKE THE SAUCE**

*1. Preheat the oven to 450°F.*

*2. In a medium bowl, combine the oil, neck bones, celery, carrots, onion, salt, and pepper. Toss until all the ingredients are coated. Transfer to a roasting pan and roast, uncovered, for 30 minutes, or until all the vegetables and bones are nicely browned. Transfer the contents of the pan to a 2-quart or larger saucepot, scraping out the roasting pan to capture all the brown bits.*

*3. Add the red wine to the pot and cook over high heat until the liquid has reduced by half. Add the Brown Sauce, stock, garlic, shallots, and peppercorns and bring to a boil. Reduce to a simmer and cook for 2 hours. (When the sauce has cooked for about 1½ hours, begin preparing the vegetables and potatoes.)*

**TO PREPARE THE LAMB AND VEGETABLES**

*1. Reduce the oven temperature to 400°F.*

*2. In a small bowl, combine the dried oregano, garlic powder, 1 teaspoon of the salt and ¼ teaspoon of black pepper for the lamb and mix well. Thoroughly coat the lamb with this dry rub. Refrigerate and let the lamb marinate for about 10 minutes.*

*(continued)*

Two 18- to 20-ounce New Zealand lamb racks, frenched

6 tablespoons olive oil blend (3 parts canola oil to 1 part olive oil)

6 slices white bread, finely chopped in a food processor

1 tablespoon chopped garlic

1 tablespoon chopped fresh oregano

1 tablespoon chopped fresh rosemary

1 tablespoon chopped fresh flat-leaf parsley

¼ cup grated Romano cheese

¼ cup unsalted (½ stick), melted

Crusty Rosemary Potatoes (page 202)

Roasted Vegetables (page 202)

*3. Heat 4 tablespoons of the oil in a large sauté pan over medium-high heat.*

*4. Gently place the lamb in the hot oil, top side down. Cook until the top side is nicely browned. Flip the racks and brown the bottoms. Remove and transfer to a sheet pan, or pans as necessary.*

*5. In a medium bowl, combine the remaining 2 tablespoons oil, remaining 1 teaspoon salt, remaining ¼ teaspoon black pepper, the bread, garlic, oregano, rosemary, parsley, cheese, and butter. Slather a generous amount of this mixture on top of the chop portion of each rack.*

*6. Bake to the desired doneness. We recommend medium-rare; about 10 to 15 minutes. Remove from the oven and set aside.*

*7. Prepare the Roasted Vegetables (page 202) and Crusty Rosemary Potatoes (page 201) as directed in the recipes.*

*8. When the vegetables and potatoes have about 7 to 8 minutes left to cook, transfer the lamb racks to the sheet pans with the vegetables and potatoes to reheat the lamb. Remove from the oven and serve.*

TO FINISH THE DISH

*1. Strain the sauce and add the olives and sun-dried tomatoes. Return to the pot and cook for 2 to 3 minutes. Add the butter right before you're ready to serve.*

*2. Spread the roasted vegetables along with rosemary potatoes in the center of a large serving platter. Slice the lamb racks into individual chops and arrange them around the vegetables. Pour the sauce over the lamb chops, drizzling a small amount over the vegetables and potatoes. Serve immediately.*

# Roasted Filet of Beef with Cipollini Onion Sauce

*Serves 4 to 6*

## MARINATED BEEF

1 tablespoon kosher salt

1 teaspoon cracked black pepper

$^1/_2$ cup olive oil

6 cloves Roasted Garlic (page 242)

2 tablespoons thinly sliced garlic

1 tablespoon chopped fresh flat-leaf
   parsley

1 tablespoon chopped fresh rosemary

1 tablespoon chopped fresh basil

1 tablespoon chopped fresh oregano

$^1/_2$ teaspoon dried oregano

3 pounds beef tenderloin, cleaned
   and trimmed

## CIPOLLINI SAUCE (yields 2 cups)

2 tablespoons olive oil

$^1/_4$ pound cipollini onions, peeled

2 tablespoons unsalted butter

1 tablespoon chopped shallots

$^1/_2$ teaspoon kosher salt

$^1/_8$ teaspoon cracked black pepper

$^1/_4$ cup Marsala wine

When an Italian grandmother prepares Sunday dinner, she does it with gusto—and this is the type of dish she would make. The final touch—an elegantly sweet and silky cipollini onion sauce—is what puts the dish over the top. The dish makes for exceptional leftovers that keep well and reheat to the original glory—especially if you've reserved a little of the cipollini sauce.

### TO MARINATE THE BEEF

*1. In a small bowl, combine all the ingredients for the marinade, except for the meat, and mix well.*

*2. Lay the beef on a sheet pan and coat evenly all over with the marinade. Cover with plastic wrap and refrigerate overnight.*

### TO MAKE THE SAUCE

*1. Heat the olive oil for the cipollini sauce in a 2-quart or larger saucepot over high heat. Add the onions and brown well on all sides. Add the butter, shallots, salt, and pepper and sauté for 1 minute, or until the shallots are translucent. Add the wines and cook until the liquid has reduced by half.*

*2. Add the Brown Sauce and bring to a boil. Reduce to a simmer and cook for about 20 minutes. Remove the sauce from the heat and set aside.*

*(continued)*

$^{1}/_{4}$ cup red wine

2 cups Brown Sauce (page 249)

**POTATOES**

1 pound russet potatoes

1 tablespoon chopped fresh basil

$^{1}/_{3}$ cup Garlic-Herb Oil (page 243)

**ROASTED TOMATOES**

4 fresh Roma tomatoes

$^{1}/_{2}$ teaspoon kosher salt

$^{1}/_{8}$ teaspoon cracked black pepper

1 cup Carmine's Bread Crumbs (page 244)

2 tablespoons extra-virgin olive oil

2 teaspoons grated Romano cheese

**SAUTÉED MUSHROOMS**

3 tablespoons unsalted butter

1 tablespoon chopped shallots

1 pound button mushrooms, cleaned (see page 21)

$^{1}/_{4}$ cup white wine

1 tablespoon chopped fresh flat-leaf parsley

1 tablespoon chopped fresh basil

$^{1}/_{2}$ teaspoon kosher salt

$^{1}/_{8}$ teaspoon cracked black pepper

### TO MAKE THE POTATOES

*1. Preheat the oven to 350°F.*

*2. Wash and cut the potatoes crosswise into $^{3}/_{8}$-inch-thick slices. In a medium bowl, combine the potatoes, basil, and garlic-herb oil and toss to coat. Let marinate for 10 minutes, then spread the potatoes in one layer on a nonstick sheet pan. Roast for 20 to 25 minutes. Flip the slices and roast for 10 minutes more, or until the potatoes are nicely browned. Set aside to cool.*

### TO ROAST THE TOMATOES

*1. Increase the oven temperature to 400°F.*

*2. Slice each tomato in half lengthwise. Spread the tomatoes on a sheet pan, cut side up, and season with the salt and pepper. Top each tomato half with a generous amount of bread crumbs, pressing them firmly into the tomatoes. Drizzle the tomatoes with the extra-virgin olive oil and sprinkle with the grated cheese.*

*3. Bake for 15 to 18 minutes, or until the tomatoes are soft and the breading is nicely browned. Remove from the oven and set aside. Reduce the oven temperature to 350°F.*

### TO MAKE THE MUSHROOMS

*Preheat a large sauté pan over medium-high heat. Add the butter and shallots and sauté for 1 minute, or until the shallots are slightly browned. Add the mushrooms and brown well on all sides. Add the wine, parsley, basil, salt, and pepper and cook until almost dry. Remove from the heat and set aside.*

*(continued)*

## Roasted Filet of Beef with Cipollini Onion Sauce *(continued)*

**PAN-SEARED ASPARAGUS**

2 tablespoons unsalted butter

1 pound thin-stalk asparagus, ends trimmed

1/2 teaspoon kosher salt

1/8 teaspoon cracked black pepper

**FRIED SHALLOTS**

1 1/2 cups canola oil

1/4 pound shallots

1 cup all-purpose flour

1/2 teaspoon salt

1/8 teaspoon cracked black pepper

**TO PREPARE THE ASPARAGUS**

*Preheat a large sauté pan over medium-high heat. Add the butter and asparagus and sauté until the asparagus begins to pick up some color. Season with the salt and pepper. Using tongs, transfer the asparagus spears to a small sheet pan.*

**TO MAKE THE FRIED SHALLOTS**

*1. Line a plate with paper towels. Heat the canola oil in a 2-quart pot over medium-high heat. While the oil is heating, cut the shallots into very thin slices.*

*2. Mix the flour with the salt and pepper. Dredge the shallot slices in the seasoned flour and shake off any excess. When the oil is about 350°F, slide the shallots into the oil and fry until golden brown. Transfer to the paper towel–lined plate and set aside.*

**TO FINISH THE DISH**

*1. Spread out all the vegetables, except for the fried shallots, on two sheet pans, keeping each type of vegetable separate. Lay the marinated beef on a third sheet pan.*

*2. Roast the beef for 15 to 45 minutes depending on your preferred doneness (see the temperature ranges on page 162), checking the internal temperature with a meat thermometer. Remove the beef from the oven and allow it to rest for 10 minutes.*

*3. While the beef rests, briefly roast the sheet pans of vegetables. Return the pan of sauce to the stovetop and gradually reheat the sauce over medium-low heat.*

*4. Cut the beef into 1/2-inch-thick slices. Keep the slices together.*

*(continued)*

## Roasted Filet of Beef with Cipollini Onion Sauce *(continued)*

*Remove the vegetables from the oven, and place the potatoes lengthwise down the center of a serving platter. Layer the sliced filet in the same way, on top of the potatoes. Arrange the vegetables around the edges of the platter, leaving a little space at the front of the platter. Pour the sauce in the space at the front and drizzle some on top of the meat. Garnish with the fried shallots and serve.*

# Beef Involtini

*Serves 4 to 6*

**FILLING**

- ½ pound sourdough bread, crust removed, bread cut into ½-inch cubes
- 3 cups chicken stock
- ¼ cup olive oil
- 2 tablespoons chopped garlic
- ½ cup finely diced white onions
- ½ cup julienned prosciutto
- ½ cup raisins
- 2 tablespoons chopped fresh basil
- 2 tablespoons chopped fresh flat-leaf parsley
- 1 cup grated Romano cheese
- ½ cup shredded aged provolone cheese

**SAUCE**

- ¼ cup olive oil
- ½ cup finely diced white onions
- ½ cup finely diced carrots
- ½ cup finely diced celery
- 1 tablespoon sliced garlic
- 1 cup red wine
- ¼ cup pepperoncini brine (from a jar of pepperoncini peppers)

Sometimes called braciole in Southern Italy, these beef rolls are amazingly delectable concoctions that involve smashing beef slices thin (and tenderizing them in the process) and then rolling the slices up around a mouthwatering filling full of savory ingredients. We serve ours with a masterpiece tomato ragu redolent of an herb garden, perfectly in sync with the hearty flavor of the beef.

### TO MAKE THE FILLING

*1. In a small bowl, combine the bread for the stuffing with 2 cups of the chicken stock.*

*2. Heat the olive oil in a large sauté pan over medium-high heat and add the garlic and onions. When they begin to brown, add the prosciutto and sauté for 2 to 3 minutes.*

*3. Add the remaining 1 cup chicken stock, the raisins, basil, and parsley and cook until the liquid has reduced by one-quarter.*

*4. Reduce the heat to low. Add the soaked bread and both cheeses and mix well. Remove from the heat and transfer to a shallow dish, spreading the ingredients out evenly. Refrigerate, uncovered, for 1 hour, or until thoroughly chilled.*

### TO MAKE THE SAUCE

*1. Heat the olive oil in a large sauté pan over medium-high heat. Add the onions, carrots, celery, and garlic, mix well to combine, and sauté until nicely browned.*

*(continued)*

# Beef Involtini *(continued)*

2 cups canned whole, peeled Italian plum tomatoes with purée

2 cups Brown Sauce (page 249)

2 tablespoons chopped fresh flat-leaf parsley

2 teaspoons chopped fresh rosemary

1 teaspoon chopped fresh thyme

2 tablespoons chopped fresh basil

1½ teaspoons chopped fresh oregano

1 teaspoon kosher salt

¼ teaspoon cracked black pepper

1½ cups chicken stock

1 dried bay leaf

**BEEF**

2½ pounds beef top round, cut into 2 narrow slices, then pounded ⅜-inch thick

1 teaspoon kosher salt

¼ teaspoon cracked black pepper

½ cup olive oil blend (3 parts canola oil to 1 part olive oil)

*2. Add the wine and pepperoncini brine, bring to a boil, and cook until the liquid has reduced by half.*

*3. Reduce the heat to medium, add the rest of the sauce ingredients, and cook for about 15 minutes. The sauce should reduce just slightly. Pour the cooked sauce into a deep 9 x 13-inch baking dish (or similar size).*

## TO PREPARE THE BEEF ROLLS

*1. Preheat the oven to 350°F.*

*2. Lay the beef out on a cutting board. Season it lightly with salt and cracked black pepper on both sides.*

*3. Remove the stuffing from the refrigerator and divide it in half. Spread half of the stuffing on top of each piece of beef, spreading it to about ½ inch from the edges. Roll each piece up along the short side.*

*4. Beginning at one end, tie each roll with butcher's twine about every 2 inches along the length of the roll.*

*5. Heat the olive oil blend in a large sauté pan over medium-high heat. Place both beef rolls in the pan. Sear the rolls all the way around until as much of the outside surface as possible is nicely browned.*

*6. Transfer the beef rolls to the pan with the sauce. Cover with aluminum foil and bake for 1 hour and 15 minutes. Remove from the oven and let the beef cool. Refrigerate, covered, for 24 hours; this allows the flavors to marry and stuffing to set.*

## TO FINISH THE DISH

*1. Preheat the oven to 350°F.*

*2. Heat the cooked beef rolls in the pan with the sauce for 30 to 40 minutes, or until entirely heated through. Gently remove the twine from both rolls and, using a very sharp knife, carefully cut each roll into 1-inch slices. Shingle the slices on a serving platter and top with the sauce the rolls were heated with. Serve immediately.*

# Side Dishes

The best Italian meals are more than just a collection of recipes; they are thoughtful compositions, with each course complementing the others. The Italian name for side dishes—*contorni*—actually reinforces that notion. It translates to "contours," because the dishes are meant to fill out the edges of the meal, helping shape it and creating a more complete culinary picture.

The side dishes themselves are traditionally focused on fresh vegetables and herbs picked from local gardens. The elegant simplicity that marks the best Italian cooking is on full display in the cuisine's side dishes, and Carmine's makes the most of that uncomplicated nature. Our contorni include two versions of wonderful focaccia, the Italian herbed bread that is ideal for soaking up savory sauces (or fantastic as a snack between meals). We've also included some of our guests' favorite sides, with rich deep vegetable flavors and compelling blends of spices and herbs.

We've chosen the recipes for this chapter carefully, so that all of them can be used for more than just side dishes. In most cases, you can increase the recipe to turn it into a vegetarian main course, or you can mix and match to make up a meal comprised solely of side dishes.

The truth is, even if these play second fiddle to the *secondo* (main course), that doesn't mean we've lavished any less attention on the ideal balance of herb, spices, and other ingredients. In fact, these are all flavor indulgences, each of which packs a big taste-bud punch in a small package.

# Tomato Focaccia

*Serves 6 to 8*

**DOUGH**

1 teaspoon active dry yeast

1 teaspoon granulated sugar

3½ tablespoons olive oil blend (3 parts canola oil to 1 part olive oil), plus more for the pan

1 tablespoon chopped fresh rosemary

1 tablespoon kosher salt

1½ pounds bread flour

4 cloves Roasted Garlic (page 242)

**HERB OIL**

1 teaspoon chopped fresh flat-leaf parsley

3 tablespoons olive oil (preferably from the roasted garlic)

¼ teaspoon freshly ground black pepper

½ teaspoon dried oregano

1 tablespoon chopped garlic

½ teaspoon kosher salt

**TOPPING**

One 28-ounce can whole, peeled San Marzano tomatoes

2 tablespoons chopped fresh flat-leaf parsley

½ cup grated Romano cheese

Focaccia has been a favorite flatbread of Mediterranean cultures as far back as the ancient Greeks. Olive oil is a constant in all focaccia recipes, but other flavorful ingredients are subject to personal preference. Our's is the height of simplicity, allowing the naturally rich heartiness and unmistakable flavors of San Marzano tomatoes and grated Romano cheese to dominate.

**TO MAKE THE DOUGH**

*1. In a stand mixer equipped with a dough hook, combine 1½ cups warm tap water with the yeast, and mix on low speed until fully dissolved. Add the sugar and continue blending. Add the oil, rosemary, and salt and mix on low speed for 2 minutes.*

*2. With the mixer running, slowly add the flour until the consistency is smooth. Add the roasted garlic and mix until incorporated.*

*3. Transfer the dough to a floured work surface. Roll it into a round, smooth ball using a circular motion. Cover with a clean dishtowel and let rest for 20 minutes.*

*4. Using a rolling pin, roll out the dough, periodically dusting it with flour to prevent the dough from sticking, to the size and shape of a half sheet pan. Oil a half sheet pan. Spread the dough out on the pan, pressing it into the corners.*

**TO MAKE THE HERB OIL**

*In a small bowl, combine all of the herb oil ingredients, blending them thoroughly. Distribute the mixture evenly across the top of the dough, and refrigerate the dough, uncovered, for 3 hours.*

2 tablespoons chopped fresh basil

¹/₄ teaspoon freshly ground black pepper

1 teaspoon kosher salt

¹/₄ cup olive oil blend (3 parts canola oil to 1 part olive oil)

**GARNISH**

¹/₂ cup chopped fresh basil

¹/₂ cup chopped fresh flat-leaf parsley

¹/₄ cup grated Romano cheese

**TO MAKE THE TOPPING**

*Drain the tomatoes, gently pressing out the juice. In a medium bowl, break up the tomatoes with your hands, keeping the consistency somewhat chunky. Add the remaining topping ingredients to the bowl and mix until thoroughly incorporated.*

**TO ASSEMBLE AND BAKE THE FOCACCIA**

*1. Remove the dough from the refrigerator and re-stretch the dough back into the corners of the pan; the dough will have shrunk a bit while refrigerated.*

*2. Spread the topping evenly across the dough. Place the sheet pan in a warm area for 30 to 40 minutes, or until the dough has risen slightly above the sides.*

*3. Preheat the oven to 325°F.*

*4. In a small bowl, combine the garnish ingredients and mix to incorporate. Sprinkle the garnish liberally across the dough.*

*5. Bake the focaccia for 25 minutes. Remove from the oven and break up any bubbles in the surface. Return it to the oven and bake for an additional 5 to 10 minutes, or until the dough is golden brown.*

*6. Remove the focaccia from the oven and allow it to cool in the pan. Cut into 2-inch squares and serve warm in a large basket.*

Tomatoes in all their many forms, from fresh slices to canned and diced, are such a mainstay of Italian cooking (and especially the evolution to Italian-American cuisine) that it is perhaps a bit surprising that the tomato itself doesn't even appear in Italian writings until the sixteenth century. It is not mentioned as a prominent part of cooking until the late eighteenth century, and even then was thought to be a rather base element in the cuisine. Pity the medieval masses who never got to fully enjoy the red jewel of the garden.

The reason for this is, in large part, that the tomato was not indigenous to Europe. When it finally did make the trip to the Old World, courtesy of Spanish explorers returning from what is now South and Central America, it was only widely cultivated by Spaniards. When the fruit first made its way to Italy, there was a great deal of confusion about what exactly it was. At first it was grown strictly as an ornamental plant for its beautiful color and endearing shape. Many people actually thought the fruit was poisonous.

Experimentation being the soul of any cuisine, that opinion was bound to change. As cooks discovered the amazing potential in tomatoes, everyone at the table learned just how flavorful they could be. The response was enthusiastic, and the fruit was eventually named *pomi d'oro*, or the "golden apple." Serving it fresh at first, cooks quickly began to strip the fruit of its tough skin and bothersome seeds, and stew and sauté the chopped-up tomato. Eventually, they cooked it down even further into scintillating sauces that replaced the ubiquitous flour and meat juice "gravy."

The more they ate, the more people discovered that not all tomatoes are created equal. Cooks were turning to only the most flavorful, and also those with the least amount of seeds and the thickest flesh—both of which promised more culinary reward for less work.

Over time, the oblong plum tomato became the preferred addition to Italian cooking, with supporting roles played by the beefsteak (more in the New World than the Old) and other lesser versions when the plum tomato was unavailable. The type of plum tomato used most often throughout Italy was and is the Roma. The two names are sometimes used interchangeably, but the truth is, while all Romas are plums, not all plums are Romas. A good thing to keep in mind when shopping.

Roma tomatoes feature a fairly hearty flavor, high acidity, and come in both red and yellow varieties. The flavor is more complex than many other tomatoes and can hold up against a strong spice mix. Roma tomatoes are also appealingly fleshy, and mature quickly on the vine. However, they are actually the progeny of an even more renowned tomato.

The type of Roma most revered in Italian cooking on both sides of the Atlantic is the San Marzano. This variety is named for the region in Campania in which it was first cultivated. San Marzano tomatoes are longer and more pointed than other plum varieties, and they are a bit fleshier with fewer seeds. But what really makes this type a favorite among Italian cooks and anyone with an appetite is the distinctively sweet and luxurious flavor. They are also noticeably less acidic than other tomatoes.

Because authentic San Marzano tomatoes are

still only grown in that particular region, getting them to markets as far away as America eventually leads to the age-old question of whether fresh or canned tomatoes are better.

It's really a trick question. Fresh, fully ripe plum tomatoes can be wonderful additions to salads or cold antipasti platters, and certainly in most salads there is no substitute for fresh. The trick is that phrase, "fully ripe." Many fresh, bright red tomatoes you buy in a grocery store were picked green and allowed to ripen on the way to market. Others have been genetically modified or treated with chemicals to bloom into a seductive, rich red color regardless of actual ripeness. You can play it safe by buying organic tomatoes and especially those from local sources. Unfortunately, even in warmer areas of the country, that means having fresh tomatoes only in the summer. So, when it comes using the tomatoes out of season, or cooking them—especially for sauces—the decision between canned and fresh will tilt toward cans. Fortunately, the high acidity and general nature of tomatoes makes them some of the most ideal produce for canning.

Reputable companies can tomatoes with a minimum of processing. They use ripe produce and don't overcook the tomatoes, and they don't use unnecessary additives. These days, you can find canned tomatoes from peeled and whole to finely diced, to suit your needs regardless of the dish you're cooking. Cans of San Marzano tomatoes will usually be more difficult to find, and tend to cost more as well, but most cooks consider the difference in flavor noticeable enough to make the purchase an easy decision. Just be aware that not all canned tomatoes labeled San Marzano are actually grown in the region. The only guaranteed product are cans with a DOP label, indicating they have been certified Denominazione d'Origine Protetta by the Italian government.

When the recipe calls for fresh tomatoes, you often need to peel them or the peel can become an unattractive addition to the dish (especially in sauces). Peeling tomatoes can be a challenge unless you use a simple chef's technique.

First, score an X in the point—the end opposite the stem—of each tomato. Be sure to cut completely through the skin, but try not to cut too deeply into the flesh. The idea is just to break the tension that holds the skin in place.

Next, place the tomatoes in boiling water, making sure that you don't crowd the pot, boiling them in batches if need be. Allow them to sit in the boiling water for no longer than 45 seconds.

Using a slotted spoon, transfer the tomatoes to an ice bath—a large container filled with half ice and half cold water. (You can use a clean kitchen sink for this purpose.)

When the tomatoes cool, the skins will shrivel. Remove the tomatoes at this point and you'll be able to easily peel the skins away from the flesh. Discard the skins, remove the seeds from the tomatoes, and get started on a batch of Carmine's Marinara (page 251).

# Onion Focaccia

*Serves 6 to 8*

## DOUGH

1 teaspoon active dry yeast

1 teaspoon granulated sugar

3½ tablespoons olive oil blend (3 parts canola oil to 1 part olive oil), plus more for the pan

1 tablespoon kosher salt

5 cups bread flour

4 cloves Roasted Garlic (page 242)

## HERB OIL

⅓ cup olive oil, preferably from the roasted garlic

1 teaspoon chopped fresh flat-leaf parsley

¼ teaspoon freshly ground black pepper

½ teaspoon kosher salt

## TOPPING

¼ cup olive oil blend (3 parts canola oil to 1 part olive oil)

1 pound white onions, sliced

2 tablespoons chopped fresh basil

2 tablespoons chopped fresh flat-leaf parsley

1 teaspoon kosher salt

¼ teaspoon freshly ground black pepper

Focaccia elevates the idea of bread served with a meal, and this recipe elevates the idea of focaccia. The chewy, savory bread is essentially a custom-made platform for an onion-laden topping rich with Italian cheese. The secret to this delightful meal addition is the flavor-packed herb oil we coat the bread with before the topping goes on.

### TO MAKE THE DOUGH

*1. In a stand mixer equipped with a dough hook, combine 1½ cups warm water with the yeast and mix on low speed until fully dissolved. Add the sugar and continue mixing. Add the oil and salt and mix on low speed for 2 minutes.*

*2. With the mixer running, gradually add the flour, a little bit at a time. Add the roasted garlic and continue mixing until the garlic is incorporated and the dough is smooth.*

*3. Transfer the dough to a warm floured work surface. Roll the dough into a round ball using a circular motion. Cover the dough ball loosely with a clean dishtowel and let rest for 20 minutes.*

*4. Using a rolling pin, roll out the dough, periodically dusting it with flour to prevent sticking, to roughly the size and shape of a half sheet pan. Oil a half sheet pan and spread the dough on the pan, pressing it into the corners.*

### TO MAKE THE HERB OIL

*In a small bowl, thoroughly combine all ingredients for the herb oil. Evenly distribute the oil mixture over the top of the dough. Refrigerate the dough, uncovered, for 3 hours.*

¹/₂ cup chopped fresh basil

¹/₂ cup chopped fresh flat-leaf parsley

¹/₄ cup grated Romano cheese

### TO MAKE THE TOPPPING

*Heat the oil in a large sauté pan over medium-high heat. Add the onions, basil, parsley, salt, and pepper and sauté until the onions are translucent. Transfer the topping to a sheet pan and let cool.*

### TO PREPARE THE GARNISH

*In a small bowl, combine the basil, parsley, and grated cheese and mix well.*

### TO ASSEMBLE AND BAKE THE FOCACCIA

*1. Preheat the oven to 325°F.*

*2. Remove the dough from the refrigerator and re-stretch the dough back into the corners of the pan; the dough will have shrunk a bit while refrigerated. Evenly distribute the onion topping across the dough. Place the pan in a warm area for 30 to 40 minutes, or until the dough has risen a bit above the sides.*

*3. Sprinkle the garnish mixture over the topping. Bake the focaccia for 25 to 30 minutes. Remove from the oven and break up any bubbles on the surface. Bake for 5 to 10 minutes more, or until the dough is golden brown. Remove from the oven and let cool in the pan. Cut into 2-inch squares and serve warm in a napkin-lined basket.*

# Escarole, Pancetta, and Cannellini Beans

*Serves 4 to 6*

1/4 pound pancetta, finely diced

1/4 cup olive oil blend (3 parts canola oil to 1 part olive oil)

1/4 cup sliced garlic

2 tablespoons chopped fresh basil

2 tablespoons chopped fresh flat-leaf parsley

1 1/2 pounds escarole, cleaned and cut into 2 1/2-inch pieces

1 teaspoon kosher salt

1/4 teaspoon cracked black pepper

1 cup canned cannellini beans (Progresso brand recommended)

1 cup chicken stock

1/3 cup grated Romano cheese

Like spinach and bacon, escarole and pancetta are a natural combination, one that offers basic but enticingly sturdy and savory flavors. The herb and spice mix used in this recipe is modest because there isn't much need to supplement the hearty natural flavors. A helping of white beans and a kiss of Romano cheese complete this side dish and make it totally satisfying.

*1. Heat a large (at least 8-quart) pot over medium-high heat. Add the pancetta and sauté until it begins to pick up color. Add the oil and sliced garlic and sauté until browned.*

*2. Add the basil, parsley, and escarole and sauté for 2 to 3 minutes; the escarole should just begin to wilt.*

*3. Add the salt and pepper, beans, and chicken stock and bring to a boil. Cook over high heat for 4 to 5 minutes, or until the escarole is tender. Mix in the grated cheese and serve.*

# Broccoli Rabe

*Serves 4 to 6*

¹/₂ cup olive oil blend (3 parts canola oil to 1 part olive oil)

¹/₄ cup sliced garlic

1¹/₂ pounds broccoli rabe, stems trimmed

1 ¹/₂ teaspoons kosher salt

4 cloves Roasted Garlic (page 242)

¹/₈ teaspoon cracked black pepper

¹/₂ teaspoon crushed red pepper flakes

1 cup chicken stock

Like the best side dishes, this super satisfying recipe is incredibly simple to create. Broccoli rabe has an appealing bitterness that is just tart enough to tingle the palate, but not so much as to be unappetizing. You can make this same magic with kale, collard greens, mustard, or other greens by simply substituting them for the broccoli rabe.

*1. Heat the oil in a large (at least 8-quart) pot over medium-high heat. Add the sliced garlic and sauté until well browned.*

*2. Add the broccoli rabe, salt, roasted garlic, black pepper, and red pepper flakes. Do not move the greens for 1 to 2 minutes after adding them to the pan to allow the surfaces of the vegetable to brown.*

*3. Turn the broccoli rabe and cook for 1 minute more. Add the chicken stock, bring to a boil, and cook for 2 to 3 minutes, or until the stems of the broccoli rabe become slightly tender.*

*4. Transfer the broccoli rabe to a large serving bowl, top with the broth, and serve.*

# Mashed Potatoes

*Serves 4 to 6*

4 pounds russet potatoes, peeled and cubed

1 tablespoon chopped garlic

6 cloves Roasted Garlic (page 242)

1 cup heavy cream

$1/4$ pound ($1/2$ stick) unsalted cold butter, cut into $1/2$-inch pieces

1 cup whole milk

1 tablespoon kosher salt

$1/2$ teaspoon cracked black pepper

We serve our mashed potatoes with the smoky sweet kiss of roasted garlic and lots of rich cream and butter. The result is a side dish worthy of main-course attention, but not to worry, this is still a perfect partner to meat, veal, and chicken dishes of all kinds.

*1. Place the potatoes in a small stockpot, cover them with cold water, and bring to a boil over high heat., Reduce to a simmer and cook until the potatoes are fork-tender, 15 to 20 minutes.*

*2. While the potatoes are cooking, combine the rest of the ingredients in a large saucepan over medium-high heat. Bring to a boil, then reduce the heat to just keep the mixture warm.*

*3. When the potatoes are tender, drain and allow them to air-dry for 1 to 2 minutes. Mash the potatoes, then add the cream mixture, and incorporate just until smooth; do not overmix. Serve warm.*

# Sautéed Spinach

*Serves 4 to 6*

½ cup olive oil

4 cloves Roasted Garlic (page 242)

2 tablespoons sliced garlic

1 ½ pounds spinach, well rinsed and dried

1 teaspoon kosher salt

¼ teaspoon cracked black pepper

Spinach is a wonderful salad green, but the fresh, vibrant flavor in this healthy garden standard is at its best when cooked quickly and lightly. We sauté our spinach side dish just a whisper past wilting, so that the leafy vegetable still has an appealingly sturdy texture. This dish is proof positive that you don't have to slave away in the kitchen to make an exceptional main course accompaniment.

*1. Heat the olive oil in a large pot over medium-high heat. Add both garlics and sauté until nicely browned.*

*2. Stir in the spinach. Just as the leaves begin to wilt, add the salt and pepper and stir to incorporate. Immediately drain the excess liquid, lightly squeezing the spinach to help drain.*

*3. Transfer to a serving dish and serve hot.*

# Garlic Bread

*Serves 4 to 6*

One 2½- to 2¾-pound
Compobasso sourdough bread
(large round peasant bread with
crispy, charred crust)

1½ cups Garlic Butter (page 248)

⅓ cup grated Romano cheese

Like so many Italian side dishes—especially the side dishes at Carmine's—this one uses the simplest of ingredients to create a supremely pleasing taste sensation. Our garlic bread is versatile, delicious, and fabulously quick to make. So much so, that we can't imagine that you wouldn't want to serve it at every meal.

*1. Preheat the oven to broil.*

*2. Cut the bread in half to create two semicircular loaves. Cut each loaf into 1-inch slices; it should yield about 10 to 12 slices.*

*3. Spread the slices out on a sheet pan (use two sheet pans if necessary) and place under the broiler until lightly toasted, 15 to 30 seconds. Flip each slice and lightly toast the opposite side. Remove from the broiler and let cool.*

*4. Spread 2 to 3 tablespoons of garlic butter on each slice, depending on the size (the end slices will take about 2 tablespoons, while the center slices will need about 3 tablespoons).*

*5. Sprinkle the grated cheese over the slices and return them to the sheet pan(s).*

*6. Bake for 10 to 12 minutes, or until evenly toasted and the butter is completely melted. Serve hot.*

# Garlic-Roasted Broccoli

*Serves 4 to 6*

3/4 cup olive oil

3 tablespoons sliced garlic

1 1/2 pounds broccoli, cleaned, stems trimmed

4 cloves Roasted Garlic (page 242)

1/2 teaspoon kosher salt

1/8 teaspoon cracked black pepper

1 cup chicken stock

Broccoli is a sturdy and healthy addition to the dinner table, but its flavor is subdued; most of the interest in the vegetable lies in its crunchy texture. That is, until you combine it with some salty spices and the memorable essence of roasted garlic. Suddenly you have taste complexity that slots right in next to any Italian main dish you might serve.

*1. Heat the olive oil in a large sauté pan over medium-high heat. Add the sliced garlic and sauté until well browned.*

*2. Add the broccoli, roasted garlic, salt, and pepper. Do not move the broccoli for 1 to 2 minutes after adding it to the pan to allow the surfaces of the vegetable to brown.*

*3. Turn the broccoli and cook for 1 minute more.*

*4. Add the chicken stock and bring to a boil. Cook for 3 to 4 minutes, or until the broccoli stems become slightly tender. Transfer the broccoli—being sure to include all the garlic—to a serving bowl and serve hot.*

# Crusty Rosemary Potatoes

*Serves 4*

- 2 pounds red bliss potatoes, halved
- 4 tablespoons (½ stick) unsalted butter
- 1 tablespoon chopped garlic
- ½ teaspoon kosher salt
- ¼ teaspoon cracked black pepper
- 1 tablespoon chopped fresh oregano
- 1 tablespoon chopped fresh flat-leaf parsley
- 1 tablespoon chopped fresh rosemary
- ¼ cup grated Romano cheese
- ¼ cup olive oil
- ½ cup finely diced white onion
- 1 teaspoon dried oregano

Flavorful red potatoes roasted with pieces of garlic, and that sturdiest of herbs—rosemary—are just the thing for a meaty meal, such as our Porterhouse Pizzaiola (page 161), or even rich chicken dishes with heavier sauces, like Chicken Marsala (page 158). The "crust" on these potatoes comes courtesy of roasted shredded cheese.

*1. Preheat the oven to 400°F.*

*2. In a large bowl, combine all the ingredients and toss to coat. Spread the potatoes out evenly across a baking sheet.*

*3. Bake for 25 to 30 minutes, or until tender and lightly browned.*

# Roasted Vegetables

*Serves 4*

1 zucchini, cut into thin wedges

1 yellow squash, seeded and cut into thin wedges

1 eggplant, cut into thin wedges

1 medium carrot, halved lengthwise and cut into 8 pieces

1 red bell pepper, cored, seeded, and cut into 6 pieces

2 red onions, peeled and cut into $1/2$-inch slices

2 medium portobello mushroom, gills and stems removed, caps quartered

1 fennel bulb, cored and cut into 8 wedges

1 cup olive oil blend (3 parts canola oil to 1 part olive oil)

1 tablespoon chopped garlic

$1/2$ teaspoon dried oregano

1 tablespoon chopped fresh oregano

1 tablespoon chopped fresh rosemary

1 tablespoon chopped fresh flat-leaf parsley

2 teaspoons kosher salt

$1/4$ teaspoon cracked black pepper

Roasting any vegetable usually brings out a characteristic sweetness as the sugars in the vegetable caramelize. The other deeper, savory flavors ride on top of the sweetness to create a side dish that is remarkably satisfying—especially when it sits next to a cut of meat or a thick, meaty pasta sauce. The textures also bring a lot of interest to this dish

*1. Preheat the oven to 400°F.*

*2. In a large bowl, combine all the ingredients and toss to coat. Let marinate for 10 minutes.*

*3. Spread the marinated vegetables on a baking sheet. Roast for 25 to 30 minutes, or until tender and lightly browned.*

# Desserts

There is no better way to end a meal—especially a wonderful Italian meal like grandma would have made—than with just a touch of something sweet. A little dolce is a wonderful punctuation mark on the main course, and it should be just as memorable.

Fortunately, the sweet treats born of an Italian kitchen feature unique combinations of flavors and textures that make this course every bit as strong a performer as what is served before it. Surprisingly, these most decadent of recipes have not always been a large part of the cuisine. Desserts in Italy were usually reserved for special occasions, and the exalted status of those sweets that were served ensured that each was incredible in its own right. From humble beginnings came the luscious classics like heavenly tiramisu and the simple, but luxuriously silky, semifreddo. Italian-Americans built on those favorites to fill out the dessert end of restaurant menus.

Most of our desserts, like our other courses, are family-style portions that can feed a crowd. That makes them not only perfect large-group final courses, but also ideal as stand-alone indulgences for special celebrations such as birthdays or anniversaries. Our Titanic Sundae is perhaps the most popular dessert on our menu, but it doesn't keep. Leftover cheesecake and our Mixed Berry Crostata, on the other hand, can be refrigerated for up to a week for super delicious weeknight desserts. Whichever you choose, don't be surprised if you find yourself wishing that you had just skipped right over the main course!

# Mini Chocolate Cannoli

*Serves 4 to 6 (about 16)*

1 pound fresh ricotta cheese

³/₄ cup plus 2 tablespoons confectioners' sugar

¹/₈ teaspoon ground cinnamon

¹/₂ teaspoon pure vanilla extract

1¹/₂ teaspoons orange zest

¹/₂ cup mini chocolate chips

¹/₄ cup finely diced candied citron

16 chocolate-dipped mini cannoli shells

1 cup coarsely chopped pistachios

Like so many specialties of Italian cooking, cannolis are a simple treat that lend themselves to many variations. The singular form, *cannolo*, translates to "little tube." That perfectly describes this light and delicate dessert. The idea is to fill a cylinder of fried puff pastry with a lightly sweet, temptingly smooth cheese mixture. We make ours in a miniature form, each only one or two bites—ideal to end a large and heavy meal.

*1. In the bowl of a stand mixer equipped with a paddle attachment, combine the first seven ingredients, reserving 2 tablespoons of the confectioners' sugar. Beat on medium-low speed until smooth.*

*2. Spoon the filling into a pastry bag fitted with a medium tip. Pipe the filling into both ends of each cannoli shell until the shells are completely full.*

*3. Dip each end of each cannoli into the chopped pistachios and arrange on a serving platter. Dust with the reserved confectioners' sugar and serve.*

# THE ITALIAN PANTRY: A SIP OF THE MIGHTY *DIGESTIVO*

As the name suggests, the Italian after-dinner digestivos are meant to promote good digestion. Keeping a bottle or two on hand is the sign of a good host.

When it comes to digestivos, a little goes a long way. They are served in small glasses and meant to be slowly sipped. These drinks vary between the sweet and far less so, but all are relatively high in alcohol.

**Grappa:** Grappa can be an acquired taste. A distant cousin of brandy, Grappa is a clear liquor that packs a punch thanks to its high alcoholic content. It is strongly aromatic with slight herbal notes. Real Grappa is only made in Italy, and given how little is drunk at each sitting, it's worth paying a higher price for a notable bottle imported from one of the renowned vintners, such as Jacopo Poli and Nardini. Many wineries also produce their own grappa.

**Strega:** This herbal liquor is a lovely yellow color courtesy of saffron. Italian for "witch," Strega is a wickedly strong drink on par with Grappa. It features a lightly sweet flavor that includes a strong anise tone and hints of mint, pine, and herbs.

**Amaro and Other Bitters:** Amaro translates to "bitter" and that is exactly what it is. The taste follows the name, featuring a pleasantly bitter flavor with notes of herbs and citrus. Perhaps the most well-known Amaro in America is Fernet Branca, but there are many other quality producers worth trying, including Nonino and Averna.

**Sambuca:** Sambuca's signature strong, sweet, licorice flavor and aroma is a product of the star anise seed. It has a long history as the after-dinner drink of choice in famous Italian restaurants throughout America. It is traditionally served with three coffee beans floating in the liquor, said to represent health, happiness, and good fortune.

**Limoncello:** This Southern Italian creation is a lemon-flavored digestivo drunk straight as a special after-dinner treat, or used in cooking many different Italian desserts. The best part? You can make your own with our simple recipe:

*10 whole lemons*
*1 liter vodka*
*3 cups sugar*

*1. Thoroughly wash the lemons under cool water. Using a vegetable peeler, remove only the yellow peel, being careful to avoid the bitter white pith.*

*2. Place the peels in an extra-large mason jar and add the vodka. Screw the lid on the jar and store in a cool, dark area such as a cupboard. Gently shake the jar twice a week.*

*3. After 3 weeks, the liquid should have yellowed. Strain it through cheesecloth stretched over a bowl, and return the strained vodka to the jar.*

*4. In a large pitcher, combine the sugar with 3 cups warm water and stir until the sugar has completely dissolved. Let cool, and then add this Simple Syrup* to the vodka in the jar. Tighten the lid on the jar and shake vigorously. Refrigerate for 2 to 3 days before serving chilled.

A little homemade limoncello in a small decorative bottle is often given as a gift in Southern Italy. You can dial down the potency and up the sweetness by adding more of the Simple Syrup. The limoncello should be stored in the refrigerator, where it will keep for up to a year.

# Chocolate Torta

*Serves 8 to 10*

1 cup heavy cream

3 tablespoons confectioners' sugar

4 teaspoons pure vanilla extract

10 ounces semisweet chocolate chunks or chips

$^1/_2$ pound plus 4 tablespoons (2$^1/_2$ sticks) cold unsalted butter, cut into large cubes

3 extra-large eggs

$^1/_2$ cup plus 2 tablespoons granulated sugar

$^1/_4$ cup freshly brewed espresso, cooled

2 tablespoons coffee-flavored liqueur, preferably Kahlua (optional)

4 large strawberries, hulled and sliced

Cooks on the Italian island of Capri perfected this flourless chocolate cake. It is heavenly stuff, with a mysterious and alluring texture that seems to melt on the tongue, offering an intense "chocolate-ness" that can satisfy the deepest of chocolate cravings. When our torta gets very cold, it becomes almost as dense as a chocolate bar. If it has been in the refrigerator longer than two hours, we always recommend you let the torta come to room temperature before serving, which may take up to three hours, so that the consistency is more like a velvety brownie.

*1. In the bowl of a stand mixer equipped with a whisk attachment, combine the cream, 2$^2/_3$ tablespoons of the confectioners' sugar, and 1 teaspoon of the vanilla. Beat on medium to start with and increase to high when the cream thickens, beating until soft peaks form. Transfer to a bowl and refrigerate until ready to use.*

*2. Add an inch or two of water in the bottom of a double boiler (or in a 2-quart pot). Bring to a gentle boil over medium-high heat, and combine the chocolate and butter in the top of the double boiler, or in a stainless steel bowl set over the pot of simmering water. As the chocolate and butter melt, mix to blend them. When they are completely incorporated, remove the double boiler or pot from the heat, and set aside covered with a dish towel to keep the mixture warm.*

*3. Preheat the oven to 300°F.*

*(continued)*

## Chocolate Torta *(continued)*

*4. In the bowl of the stand mixer equipped with the whisk attachment, whip the eggs on high speed for 3 minutes. Add the granulated sugar and whip for 3 minutes more.*

*5. Add the espresso, coffee liqueur, and the remaining 3 teaspoons vanilla and beat until they are incorporated into the sugar and egg mixture. Remove the bowl from the mixer and gradually fold in the chocolate until the mixture is smooth and evenly mixed.*

*6. Pour the mixture into an 8-inch round cake pan, or a 5 x 10-inch baking pan. Cover with aluminum foil and place the pan in a sheet pan with high sides.*

*7. Fill the sheet pan with about 1 inch of water and place the pans in the oven. Bake the torta for 1½ hours, or until the center is just firm. Periodically check the water bath to ensure it does not go dry, and add water as necessary.*

*8. When the torta is firm with very little jiggle in the center when the pan is jostled, remove the pan from the water bath and let the torta cool for 15 minutes. Cover with plastic wrap and refrigerate until cold and firm, 2 to 3 hours.*

*9. When cool, slice the torta with a knife dipped in hot water and wiped dried on a towel (for ease of cutting). Serve each slice with a dollop of whipped cream, a few sliced strawberries, and sprinkle with some of the remaining confectioners' sugar.*

# Titanic Ice Cream Sundae

*Serves 8 to 10*

1/4 cup hazelnuts, shelled and skinned

Four 1/2-inch-thick slices fresh pineapple, drained

3 tablespoons unsalted butter, melted

2 tablespoons packed light brown sugar

2 cups heavy cream

1/2 cup confectioners' sugar

1 tablespoon pure vanilla extract

1/2 Chocolate Torta (page 212)

3 large scoops chocolate ice cream

3 large scoops vanilla ice cream

2 bananas

5 large strawberries, hulled and sliced

3/4 cup store-bought hot fudge sauce

4 rolled wafer cookies

There are ice cream sundaes and then there is the Titanic. The king of our dessert menu is the Titanic, combining a spectacular chocolate base with ice cream galore, pineapple, and fresh strawberries. This is a creation meant for a birthday party or other special occasion—although you can go ahead and use it for a splashy finish to your next dinner party.

*1. Preheat the oven to 350°F. Line a sheet pan with parchment paper.*

*2. Spread the hazelnuts on a separate, small sheet pan and toast in the oven for 5 to 7 minutes, until lightly browned, checking them often to avoid burning. Let the nuts cool and then coarsely chop them. Set aside.*

*3. Quarter each pineapple slice and combine in a small bowl with the butter and brown sugar. Toss until the pineapple is well coated. Spread on the lined sheet pan. Bake for 20 to 30 minutes, or until nicely caramelized. Remove from the oven and let cool.*

*4. In the bowl of a stand mixer equipped with a whisk attachment, combine the cream, confectioners' sugar, and vanilla. Whip on high until the cream thickens, then reduce to medium until stiff peaks form. Transfer to a bowl and refrigerate until ready to use.*

*5. When you're ready to serve the Titanic, place the torta in the center of a large serving platter. Place 3 scoops of ice cream in a line on top of the torta. Place the 3 remaining scoops of ice cream on top of the first, and slightly compress to make a stable structure and keep the scoops together.*

*(continued)*

*6. Cut the bananas lengthwise and place on either side of the torta. Using a spatula, spread the whipped cream on either side of the ice cream, leaving a small window through which the ice cream can be seen.*

*7. Add a layer of whipped cream on the top to create a boat shape and smooth again. Sprinkle the caramelized pineapple and sliced strawberries evenly across the top and sides of the whipped cream. Microwave or heat the fudge sauce in a microwave-safe glass measuring cup or bowl until warm and pourable.*

*8. Drizzle the hot fudge on top and sprinkle the chopped hazelnuts all over the sundae. Stick in the rolled wafer cookies to resemble stacks on a ship. Serve immediately before the ice cream melts.*

# Carmine's Tiramisu

*Serves 6 to 8*

### LADYFINGER CAKE

2 tablespoons unsalted butter, for greasing the pans

4 extra-large eggs

$1/4$ cup granulated sugar

$1/4$ teaspoon pure vanilla extract

$1/2$ cup all-purpose flour

### ZABAGLIONE

6 extra-large egg yolks

$1/2$ cup granulated sugar

$3/4$ cup Marsala wine

### FILLING

1 cup heavy cream

$1/2$ cup confectioners' sugar

1 teaspoon pure vanilla extract

1 cup mascarpone cheese

2 tablespoons Marsala wine

1 cup fresh brewed espresso, cooled

$1/4$ cup coffee-flavored liqueur

4 ounces semisweet chocolate, shaved

Sprinkle a cloud with sugar and cocoa and you pretty much have the beginnings of a great tiramisu. Tiramisu translates to "pick me up," and if the strong coffee used to saturate our light-as-air cake doesn't give you a jolt, the rich double layer of sweet, silky filling should at least elevate your taste buds to another level.

### TO MAKE THE CAKE

*1. Preheat the oven to 350°F. Grease two 6-inch springform pans with the butter. Line the bottom of each pan with a disk of parchment paper, and grease the parchment paper.*

*2. In the bowl of a stand mixer equipped with a whip attachment, combine the eggs, sugar, and vanilla for the ladyfinger cake and blend on medium-high speed until the mixture doubles in volume. Add the flour, and blend on low speed until incorporated.*

*3. Divide the batter evenly between the prepared springform pans. Bake for 12 to 15 minutes, or until the cakes are just cooked and begin to pull away from the side of the pans. Remove from the oven and let cool. Once cool, remove the cakes from the pans, peel off the parchment paper, and set aside.*

### TO MAKE THE ZABAGLIONE AND FILLING

*1. In a stainless steel bowl, whisk together all the zabaglione ingredients. Bring about 1 inch of water to a boil in a 2-quart pot over medium-high heat. Reduce to a simmer (the water in*

*(continued)*

the pot should be kept at a low simmer and should never come in contact with the bowl on top). Place the stainless steel bowl with the zabaglione mixture over the pot and whisk vigorously for 10 to 12 minutes, or until the volume of the mixture increases and becomes fluffy; the mixture should form soft peaks that hold their shape for several seconds. Remove the bowl from the heat and set aside.

2. In the bowl of the stand mixer equipped with a whisk attachment, combine the cream, confectioners' sugar, and vanilla for the filling. Beat on high speed until the cream begins to thicken and then reduce to medium until the texture is fluffy. Refrigerate until ready to use.

3. In a separate bowl of the stand mixer equipped with the paddle attachment, beat the mascarpone on medium speed until smooth. Add the Marsala and beat until incorporated. Gently fold the mixture into the zabaglione.

4. Use a rubber spatula to carefully fold the whipped cream mixture into the zabaglione. Gently fold it in just until incorporated and the filling is smooth; do not overmix.

## TO ASSEMBLE THE TIRAMISU

1. In a shallow pan, combine the espresso and coffee liqueur and mix until blended. Carefully lay one of the ladyfinger disks in the liquid, until it is soaked. Flip the cake and let it soak until the opposite side is saturated.

2. Place the soaked ladyfinger cake in a medium, round serving bowl and top with half of the filling. Smooth the filling with a spatula and sprinkle with half of the chocolate shavings.

*3. Soak the second ladyfinger cake in the same way, and place it on top of the first. Spread the remaining filling evenly over the top of the cake, and sprinkle with the remainder of the chocolate shavings.*

*4. Cover the serving bowl with plastic wrap and refrigerate for at least 6 hours, and preferably overnight, before serving.*

# New York–Style Cheesecake

*Serves 6 to 8*

## CRUST

$^1/_2$ pound graham crackers, finely crushed

$^1/_4$ pound (1 stick) unsalted butter, melted

$^1/_4$ cup granulated sugar

## FILLING

3 pounds cream cheese, softened

2 cups granulated sugar

$4^1/_2$ teaspoons fresh lemon juice

Zest of 1 lemon

3 teaspoons pure vanilla extract

$^3/_4$ teaspoon kosher salt

6 extra-large eggs

Our founder, Artie Cutler, was a New York City guy through and through. He loved a good bagel, the kind you can only get in New York City. For dessert, Artie always turned to another New York classic: New York Cheesecake. A satin texture and classic graham cracker crust make this one of the most popular desserts on the Carmine's menu.

### TO MAKE THE CRUST

*1. Preheat the oven to 350°F.*

*2. In a small bowl, combine the ingredients for the crust. Mix well, so that all the graham cracker crumbs are moistened.*

*3. Coat a 12-inch springform pan with nonstick cooking spray (or use a nonstick pan). Line the bottom of the pan with parchment paper cut to fit.*

*4. Spread the graham cracker mixture evenly over the bottom of the pan and press with the back of a spoon to firm the crust down into a solid, even layer. Bake for 5 to 7 minutes, until lightly browned. Remove and set aside to cool.*

### TO MAKE THE FILLING

*1. Reduce the oven temperature to 300°F.*

*2. In the bowl of a stand mixer equipped with a paddle attachment, blend the cream cheese on medium speed for 3 to 5 minutes, or until the cheese is soft and smooth. Add the sugar, lemon juice, zest, vanilla, and salt and continue blending until the mixture is smooth.*

*3. Scrape down the sides of the bowl. Blending on low, add the eggs one at a time, fully incorporating each egg before adding the next.*

*4. Pour the filling over the graham cracker crust. Place the springform pan in a sheet pan with high edges. Place in the oven and fill the sheet pan with about 1 inch of water. Bake for about 1 hour and 15 minutes, or until a toothpick inserted into the center of the cheesecake comes out clean. Periodically check the sheet pan and add water as necessary.*

*5. Remove the springform pan from the water bath and let cool for 30 minutes. When cool, refrigerate overnight.*

*6. Run a thin knife around the edge of the cheesecake before releasing the mold. Remove the cheesecake and peel off the parchment paper before cutting and serving.*

# Italian-Style Cheesecake

*Serves 6 to 8*

## CRUST

¹/₂ pound marble pound cake, sliced into 3 to 4 pieces

¹/₄ cup semisweet chocolate chips

1¹/₂ tablespoons apricot brandy

## FILLING

2¹/₂ pounds fresh whole milk ricotta cheese

8 ounces mascarpone cheese

1¹/₂ cups granulated sugar

2 tablespoons freshly squeezed orange juice

1 tablespoon orange zest

1¹/₂ teaspoons pure vanilla extract

¹/₄ teaspoon kosher salt

8 extra-large eggs

The Italians have been making cheesecake since long before America was America. Carmine's honors the original Old World version with two classic Italian cheeses that create a slightly heavier texture and creamy flavor, but we add our own spin with a blast of citrus in the cake that gives it a fresh taste. We mount our version on a suitably crumbly, chocolate-laden crust that would be a taste delight on its own.

### TO MAKE THE CRUST

*1. Preheat the oven to 350°F.*

*2. Spread the marble cake on a sheet pan and bake for 10 minutes to dry it out. Remove and let cool for 5 minutes, then coarsely crumble the pound cake into a small bowl.*

*3. Lightly coat the inside of a round 9 x 3-inch springform pan with nonstick cooking spray. Cut a 9-inch round disk of parchment paper and line the bottom of the pan with the disk.*

*4. Press the pound cake crumbs firmly down onto the bottom of the pan to form an even layer. Evenly distribute the chocolate chips across this crust and press them into the pound cake. Drizzle the crust with the brandy.*

*5. Bake the crust for 7 to 8 minutes, or until golden brown and the chips have melted. Remove and set aside to cool.*

### TO MAKE THE FILLING

*1. Reduce the oven temperature to 300°F.*

2. *In the bowl of a stand mixer equipped with a whip attachment, combine the ricotta, mascarpone, and sugar. Blend on medium-high until smooth, 3 to 5 minutes.*

3. *Add the orange juice, zest, vanilla, and salt. Blend on medium for 1 minute to incorporate.*

4. *Add the eggs, one at a time, blending on medium until the mixture is smooth. Pour the filling into the pan.*

5. *Place the springform pan in a sheet pan with high edges. Place in the oven and fill the sheet pan with about 1 inch of water. Bake for 1 to 1½ hours, or until a toothpick inserted into the center of the cake comes out clean. Periodically check the sheet pan and add water as necessary.*

6. *Remove the springform pan from the water bath and let cool for 45 minutes. Refrigerate overnight.*

7. *Carefully remove the cheesecake from the mold and remove the parchment paper before cutting and serving.*

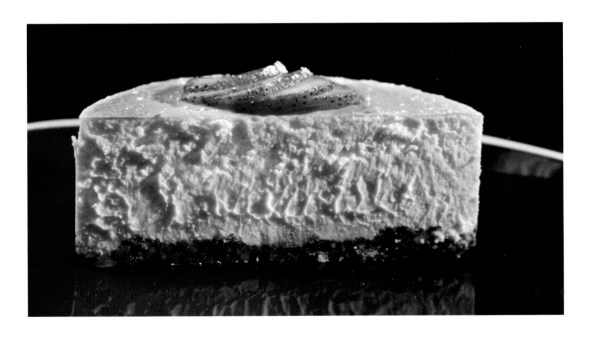

# Mixed Berry Crostata

*Serves 4 to 6*

## DOUGH

2¹/₂ cups all-purpose flour

¹/₄ cup granulated sugar

¹/₄ teaspoon kosher salt

12 tablespoons (1¹/₂ sticks) cold
  unsalted butter, sliced

¹/₂ cup whole milk

Vegetable oil, for greasing the pan

## FILLING

¹/₂ pint fresh blueberries

¹/₂ pint fresh blackberries

1 pint fresh strawberries, hulled
  and halved

¹/₄ cup plus 2 tablespoons granulated
  sugar

1 tablespoon pure vanilla extract

1¹/₂ tablespoons cornstarch

¹/₂ teaspoon orange zest

If you've ever had a really good cobbler, you've had the lesser cousin to Carmine's crostata. The crostata is a traditional Italian tart baked in the form of a pie and featuring seasonal fruit. This filling version packs in an orchard's worth of fruit, all captured in a flaky, rich crust that brings our guests back for seconds.

*1. Preheat the oven to 400°F.*

*2. In the bowl of a stand mixer equipped with a dough hook attachment, combine all the dough ingredients and blend on medium until the ingredients are incorporated and form a ball.*

*3. Remove the dough, wrap it in plastic wrap, and refrigerate for at least 1 hour to firm the dough.*

*4. In a medium bowl, combine the filling ingredients, reserving 2 tablespoons of sugar, and fold together until all the fruit is coated.*

*5. Remove the dough from the refrigerator and transfer to a work surface dusted with all-purpose flour. Flour a rolling pin and roll the dough out into a 12-inch circle.*

*6. Coat a 9-inch pie pan very lightly with vegetable oil. Center the dough on the pan and press it down into the pan.*

*7. Toss the berries again, and then pour them into the center of the dough. Gently fold the remaining dough over the filling, ensuring that at least 6 inches of the berries remain uncovered. Sprinkle the reserved 2 tablespoons sugar over the top of the crostata and bake for about 35 minutes, or until the crust is nicely browned and the fruit is bubbly. Remove the oven and let rest for 30 minutes, before slicing and serving.*

# Semifreddo with Strawberries

*Serves 6 to 8*

2 cups heavy cream

10 extra-large egg yolks

1¹/₂ cups granulated sugar

1 teaspoon pure vanilla extract

Zest and juice of 1 lemon

Zest and juice of 1 orange

¹/₂ teaspoon kosher salt

¹/₂ pint fresh strawberries,
   hulled and sliced

Just as the name describes ("half cold"), this dessert is a chilled custard with an alluring texture. Carmine's Semifreddo is all about the zing of citrus and the light and appealing fresh sweetness of strawberries. They both serve to contrast the richness of the cream- and egg-based body of the dessert.

*1. In the bowl of a stand mixer equipped with a whisk attachment, beat the cream on high speed until fairly stiff, 2 to 3 minutes. Transfer to a bowl and refrigerate until ready to use.*

*2. Fill the bottom of a double boiler or pot halfway with water and bring to a simmer. In the top of double boiler, or a stainless steel bowl that will fit over the pot, combine the egg yolks, sugar, vanilla, citrus zests and juices, and salt. Place the top of the double boiler base or bowl over the pot of simmering water and whisk the ingredients rapidly for 7 to 8 minutes, or until the mixture becomes warm and frothy.*

*3. Transfer the mixture to the bowl of the stand mixer equipped with the whisk attachment, and beat on high for 5 minutes, or until the mixture doubles in volume and cools to room temperature. Using a spatula, gently fold in the whipped cream.*

*4. Line a 10 x 5 x 4-inch or similar size loaf pan with plastic wrap, with 3 to 4 inches of extra wrap extending over the long sides; these will be overlapped to cover the semifreddo later.*

*5. Spread the strawberries on the bottom of the pan, evenly covering the bottom surface. Pour the custard into the pan, covering the strawberries. Tap the pan on a counter to eliminate any air bubbles.*

*6. Cover the top with the extra plastic wrap and gently press down. Freeze the semifreddo overnight.*

*7. When you are ready to serve, remove the semifreddo from the pan, remove the plastic wrap, and cut the semifreddo into 2-inch slices. Garnish with whatever seasonal fresh fruit you prefer, and serve.*

# CARMINE'S KITCHEN WISDOM: AW, NUTS

Nuts grow prolifically across Italy, in the wild as well as cultivated on farms, in orchards, and in large gardens. So it should come as no surprise that Italian cooking puts nuts at the center of several classic creations.

Most any nut will supply an attractive mix of healthy compounds, protein, and fiber. But, in the Italian culture, certain types are revered among others. It's just a matter of what grew where at a point in history. Once a nut grew regularly in a given region or regions, it was inevitably adopted into the cuisine and sometimes myth.

The two most valued nuts in Italy are the walnut and the pine nut. They find their way into treasured dishes, and both are also popular to eat as snacks, or simply scattered on other food such as salads. The information that follows focuses on these favorites, and others that are regularly used in Italian cooking. However, much of the information, such as how to roast, and the various uses for different nuts, can be successfully translated to other varieties, such as Brazil nuts.

No matter what nut you're using, roasting is wonderful way to amplify the natural flavor, not to mention giving the nut an inviting crunchy, crispy texture. The process is easy, although it needs to be monitored so that you don't wind up with burnt pieces. Some people use oil when roasting, but this is redundant, because most nuts already contain abundant oil. The speed at which nuts roast ensures that they don't totally dry out. Chop nuts only after they are roasted and have cooled. You can roast nuts on the stovetop in a pan, but this takes some expertise and practice. Oven roasting is the easiest and most reliable method. Here's a simple way to quickly and easily roast just about any nut.

1. Preheat the oven to 325°F.

2. Spread out the nuts on a baking sheet and place the sheet in the oven.

3. After about 4 minutes, turn the nuts with a spatula. (This isn't exacting; don't fret if you don't turn every single nut.) Check the nuts frequently throughout the roasting process to ensure that they don't burn.

4. Continue to toast until the nuts begin to take on just a bit of color. Depending on the size and thickness of the nut, roasting will take between 12 and 15 minutes. The slight brown color will be easier to discern on lighter-colored nuts such as pine nuts, but will still be detectable on darker nuts such as almonds (check them against the color of a nut you're not roasting).

5. Remove the nuts and transfer to a cookie sheet to cool.

**Hazelnuts** are dessert favorites. The nut's light, sweet flavor makes it ideal for baked goods and other sweet treats, and hazelnuts make regular appearances in the most popular biscotti recipes. It is often paired with chocolate in flourless cakes and in luscious, decadent spreads. (Nutella is the commercial version of this homemade delight.)

**Almonds** are the basis for one of the most famous Italian liqueurs, Amaretto di Saronno. The liqueur itself is named for a famous walnut cookie from the same region. Made correctly, Italian *Amaretti di Saronno* are simply heavenly, at once crisp and soft. But the nut is used for more than desserts. Although it's a standard in biscotti, it is also wonderful in many different pasta dishes; that's because the flavor of almonds complements hard cheeses, herbs, garlic, and other classic pasta sauce ingredients (it is not used as much with tomato sauces). In southern Italy, almond paste known as *marzapane* is used to make small, delicate little candies shaped like fruit and painted with food coloring.

**Walnuts** have perhaps the longest history of any nut used in Italian cuisine. Descriptions of this nut's inclusion in recipes can be found in writings centuries old. The use of walnuts in main course dishes and desserts originated in the central region of Umbria, and quickly spread out in all directions. Although they prize the nut for its ability to blend perfectly into sauces and pasta dishes, Italians are just as likely to use fresh chopped walnuts over ice cream or creamy polenta. You can use them as an accent and a garnish on top of most pastas, although they often work better with heavier or richer sauces. Walnuts are especially good paired with cream sauces, and added to Gorgonzola sauce—a tradition in the New World and the Old.

**Pine nuts** are the some of the most expensive nuts, but also some of the most richly and delicately flavored. Roasted pine nuts are frequently tossed over salads and pastas alike. Sicilians use the nut to top the classic pignoli cookies fresh out of the oven, while the entire country uses pine nuts as a base for traditional pesto. Here is a basic pesto recipe that will serve you well as a pasta sauce, bread dip, and more.

4 cups packed fresh basil leaves
3 large garlic cloves
½ cup pine nuts
1¼ cups extra-virgin olive oil
Kosher salt and fresh ground black pepper
   to taste
1 cup freshly grated Parmesan cheese

1. Combine the basil, garlic, and pine nuts in the bowl of a food processer and pulse until the ingredients are chopped.

2. With the processor on low, slowly stream in the oil. When all the oil is added, stop, taste, and season as desired with the salt and pepper.

3. Transfer to a mixing bowl and stir in the Parmesan. Use immediately.

# Almond Biscotti

*Serves 6 to 8*

1¼ cups whole roasted almonds

2 extra large eggs

2 egg yolks

1 cup plus 2 tablespoons granulated sugar, divided

1 teaspoon pure vanilla extract

1½ teaspoons almond extract

2 tablespoons orange zest

1 tablespoon anise seed

2 cups all-purpose flour

1½ teaspoons baking powder

1½ teaspoons kosher salt

**VARIATION**

You can make our version a little
fancier by microwaving 1 cup of
semisweet chocolate chips until
they melt, and then dipping
one-half of each biscotti into
the chocolate.

The secret to any biscotti is the process of baking the cookies twice. This gives them their scintillating signature crunch. Our biscotti are delicious dessert treats, but they also make wonderful light afternoon snacks, especially served with a small cup of espresso. Cool before serving.

*1. Preheat the oven to 350°F.*

*2. Spread the almonds on a sheet pan and toast in the oven for 5 to 6 minutes. Remove and let cool for 5 minutes. Transfer the almonds to the bowl of a food processor and pulse 2 to 3 times, just until the almonds are coarsely chopped.*

*3. In the bowl of a stand mixer equipped with a whisk attachment, combine the eggs, yolks, and 1 cup of the sugar (reserving the 2 tablespoons) and blend on high to the ribbon stage. Add the vanilla, almond extract, orange zest, and anise seed and blend until incorporated.*

*4. In a separate bowl, fold together the flour, baking powder, salt, and almonds. Fold the wet mixture into the dry just until smooth; do not overmix.*

*5. Coat a cookie sheet with nonstick spray. Shape the dough into an approximately 12 x 6 x 1-inch oval mound and place in the center of the cookie sheet. Sprinkle the reserved 2 tablespoons sugar on top. Bake for 20 to 25 minutes. Remove and let cool for 10 minutes.*

*6. Cut into 1-inch-thick slices. Return the slices to the cookie sheet, leaving ½ inch between each slice, and bake for 15 to 20 minutes, or until golden brown. Let cool before serving.*

Figs are a classic ingredient in Italian cuisine, and Italian culture. The Roman army included figs as part of soldiers' rations, and the country has been crazy about this fruit ever since. The fig is a chameleon in Italian cooking. Figs have made their way into antipasti, main dishes, and desserts with equal brio. That adaptability accounts for their widespread popularity.

Popularity is actually too mild a term. Immigrants from Italy brought fig trees with them and cultivated this Middle Eastern plant, even in the colder climes of the Northeast. Fig trees love heat and hate cold, so growing a fig tree in an Italian kitchen garden in America often meant taking extreme measures, including protecting the tree in heavy burlap or even burying it over winter.

Italian Americans would tell you that the fresh fruit is well worth the effort. Although avid fans are just as likely to use figs fresh as cooked, no matter how you prepare them, the complex flavor and restrained sweetness marries perfectly to a vast selection of other savory and sweet ingredients.

For Italians, the love of this fruit runs deeply into the traditions of the country and childhood memories. It's the rare Italian that hasn't experienced the wonder of a well-made fig cookie, called *cucidati* (and less often, "Sicilian X cookies"). The cookies are a standard treat for children and a signature preparation in honor of St. Joseph's Day.

No matter how you use them, picking out figs at their prime is essential to successfully incorporating them in any dish. You'll find fresh figs in late spring and autumn. The fruit varies in color depending on the variety. They range from green to purple. Instead of relying on color, hold the fig in your hand. It should be surprisingly heavy for its size, and the skin should be completely intact. Avoid any fruit with significant breaks, cracks, or obvious blemishes. The figs should be slightly soft, but not mushy (less give than a ripe avocado). Overly firm figs are not fully ripe and the flavor will be undeveloped; figs that are too soft are past their prime and the flavors may be "off." Any white sap leaking from the stem is a bad sign, as is any indication of mold on the figs.

Although they can be kept in the coldest part of your refrigerator, it's best to leave figs out with space around them for air circulation. Wherever you keep them, use figs within two days of buying them—and preferably the same day—for best results and flavor.

Italians have many uses for fresh figs, and these are often easy to prepare and delightful to serve. Mix a little mascarpone with lemon zest and add to fig halves that have been coated in honey. It's a light dessert that is ideal following a heavy pasta or a meat main course. Fresh figs are also traditionally served as an antipasto, cut and wrapped in a shawl of high-quality prosciutto.

Cooked figs are equally as wonderful on the tongue and present even more options. A classic antipasto involves wrapping whole figs or fig halves in pancetta (or bacon) slices and then roasting in a 400°F oven for 15 to 20 minutes, or until the fat in the pancetta is entirely rendered and it is crispy.

Italian cheeses are also natural complements to the flavor and texture of cooked figs, and cheese-stuffed figs are a crowd-pleasing favorite.

Chopped up, figs can be added to a salad featuring a variety of greens and savory ingredients for a surprising contrast in flavor and texture. Chopped figs can also be sautéed with sugar and butter to create a compote to spoon over ice cream, or sautéed and processed into a purée for use on a crostini with some aged Manchego or pecorino cheese. Processed figs are also a preferred filling for Italian tarts, cookies, and cakes. There's really very little that can't be made better with figs in one form or another.

Roasted figs go with cheese as an appetizer or can be served with fresh strawberries and drizzled with a high-quality balsamic vinegar for a refreshing dessert. As an alternative to roasting, you can grill figs for a unique flavor—especially if you add fruitwood chips to the coals. But roasting is often the best option for the home cook. Here's a quick way to roast figs to perfection.

1. Preheat the oven to 425°F.

2. Wash the figs and let them dry. Cut off the stems and cut each fig in half from top to bottom. Drizzle with olive oil and, if you prefer them sweet, drizzle with agave or honey.

3. Arrange the halves, cut side up, in a large glass baking dish. Sprinkle salt over the figs.

4. Bake for about 15 minutes, or until the figs pick up some color and soften.

# The Italian Kitchen Pantry

At Carmine's, we use certain basic prepared ingredients over and over again. It's not just a matter of economies of scale; these "sub-recipes" are important additions to the overall flavors in our signature dishes. In all honesty, it would be much cheaper for us to buy brown sauce or roasted peppers in bulk. But we would be sacrificing quality and giving up essential control over what goes into our dishes. That's why we make our own pantry staples, and we recommend that you do, too.

It's not hard. Most of these recipes take only minutes to prepare, cost very little, and the difference in the main recipes you create will be noticeable. As an added bonus, you'll find a million and one uses for these basics. Our Herbed Aioli (page 245) doesn't just work wonders in other recipes, it's magic on a burger, savory sandwiches of any sort, and even roasted fingerling potatoes (or fries!). Toasted Bread Crumbs (page 240) are just the thing to top a winter soup or add a bit of crunch to your next salad. No doubt, you'll find your own creative uses for these second-ary recipes. They may be walk-on players in the dramas of our larger recipes, but they can hold their own as well.

Stored correctly, some of these can keep for a long time, while others should be used in the short term. Storage usually isn't an issue, because we find that people who start making these on a regular basis find new ways to use them and go through them fairly quickly. In any case, start with the ones that make the most sense for the cooking you do, and add to your ever-growing Italian pantry.

In the early twentieth century, beans in Italy were derided as "the poor man's meat." Although it was meant as an insult, it is not a bad description. Beans of all kinds are packed with protein, fiber, and many different vitamins. They are also easy to grow, easy to cook, inexpensive to buy, and filling. So you could do a lot worse in your diet and in your recipes than using the humble bean.

As Italy's cuisine evolved and became more diverse and sophisticated, so did the use of beans in Italian kitchens. They found their way into stews, pasta dishes (Pasta e Fagioli being the most famous) and even puréed as dips or bases for other dishes. In modern Italian cooking, the bean now holds as exalted a position as any other ingredient.

The secret to a successful bean recipe is how the beans are cooked. If you're using canned, you'll usually need only to drain and rinse the beans (although the natural juice is sometimes retained to flavor the food, depending on the type of bean and the recipe) and use them without any fuss. If the beans are fresh or dried, chances are you'll be doing a bit more prep work.

The choice between canned and dried beans is a complex one. Most chefs advocate using dried when flavor is an important consideration, because the flavor of dried beans will be more pronounced. Dried beans also don't have the preservatives and other stabilizing ingredients that are often added to canned beans. They are also less expensive than canned varieties. Lastly, due to the process manufacturers use to can large batches of beans, they naturally have to overcook the beans, making them softer than many people prefer. In either case, beans are the perfect pantry staple because canned or dried, they will last a year or more.

When preparing dried beans, you'll need to soak them overnight, but no less than 8 hours. A pinch of baking soda in the soaking liquid is said to ensure the beans don't fall apart during cooking. In any case, when cooking beans don't add salt until the very end of the cooking process because it tends to make the beans harden.

The beans that follow are some of the most common in Italian cooking. But keep in mind that beans are a great way to experiment in the kitchen with very little risk. You should never hesitate to try out new types. There is an incredible number of variations, including heirloom beans, presenting a magnificent range of flavors and textures.

**Cannellini:** This is the bean of Tuscany and the reason that in the early twentieth century, Tuscans were saddled with the slightly pejorative title of *mangiafagioli,* or "bean eaters." They are large, white, and hold up well during cooking. They have a mild nutty flavor and an enchanting creamy texture inside. Cannellini are similar to Great Northern beans and navy beans, and a relative of the kidney bean—they are sometimes called white kidney beans. Like kidney beans, they require careful preparation to remove toxins in the bean that can cause gastric problems. In this case, the dried cannellini (the preferred form for cooking) should be boiled for at least 10 minutes at the start of cooking, which alleviates the need to soak them overnight. Although there are several other types of Italian white beans, cannellini is the most popular and is an essential ingredient in minestrone.

**Borlotti:** These are some of the most beautiful beans used in cooking. They are also known as cranberry beans, because of the splashes of red that mark their cream-colored shells. But as beautiful as they are, borlotti are incorporated into Italian dishes for their flavor. They offer a unique, almost meaty, savory flavor with a hint of chestnut. In this country, they are almost always used dried, and find their way into many different recipes, but are most at home and on display in a cold salad, with a simple dressing of high-quality olive oil and a splash of citrus.

**Lentils:** You may not think Italy when you think lentils, but this legume is a favorite, particularly in the south of the country. That popularity may stem from the fact that lentils are easier and quicker to cook than other beans because they don't need to be soaked overnight. The brown variety is the one most commonly used; green lentils have a stronger, peppery flavor, and take longer to cook. Colored versions are actually the lentil without its hull, and they consequently tend to fall apart during cooking.

The brown lentil, on the other hand, serves as an ideal canvas for traditional flavors such as rosemary, oregano, and even just salt and pepper. In Italian cooking, lentils are most often paired with pastas in soups. Avoid canned lentils because they become too mushy when combined in a recipe; dried lentils take so little time and effort to cook that the extra convenience of canned is not much of a benefit.

**Fava:** Considered the first bean of Italy, these are regularly eaten fresh off the vine. When you can find them, use fresh favas. They are superior to canned. Buy them still in their pods and then shell them; if the favas are young, you can use the beans with the skin on, but more likely, you'll have to remove the skins from each bean because the skins of mature beans are unappealingly leathery. Tuscans love to eat the fresh beans with pieces of pecorino and a little olive oil. Elsewhere, the bean is cooked into a wide variety of dishes to showcase an earthy, slightly sweet flavor.

**Chickpeas:** Although only grown in the south, chickpeas have found their way into regional dishes all over Italy. Fresh chickpeas are a treat although painstaking to prepare, but they are rarely available in the States. Fortunately, chickpeas lose nothing of their flavor and sturdy texture in the canning process, which is why canned chickpeas are used more frequently than dried. These are ideal in bean salads, and are traditionally coupled with pasta in the classic dish, *Pasta e Ceci*.

# Roasted Garlic and Garlic Oil

*Yields about 70 cloves and 4 cups oil*

4 cups olive oil

2 cups peeled garlic cloves
(approximately 70 cloves)

This is a two-for-one recipe that produces a couple of incredible staples that will find their way into all of your cooking. The mildly smoky, rich, and sweet flavor of roasted garlic enriches soups, stews, and pastas and is even delicious smeared on toasted bread.

*1. In a 2-quart or larger pot over medium-high heat, heat the oil until it reaches 290°F.*

*2. Add the garlic to the oil and cook for 10 to 15 minutes, or until nicely browned and thoroughly cooked throughout.*

*3. Remove the garlic and transfer to a sheet pan to cool. Remove the oil from the heat.*

*4. Strain the oil and let cool. Refrigerate in a covered container for up to 2 weeks. Refrigerate the cooled garlic in a covered container for up to 1 week.*

# Garlic-Herb Oil

*Yields 2 cups*

2 cups olive oil

1/4 cup chopped fresh garlic

1 tablespoon dried oregano

3 tablespoons fresh flat-leaf
    parsley leaves

1 1/2 teaspoons kosher salt

1/4 teaspoon cracked black pepper

Add a few traditional Italian spices to already-spectacular garlic oil and you get a base for salad dressings and other dishes with a bit more oomph than the unadorned oil.

*In a mixing bowl, combine all the ingredients and blend to incorporate. Transfer to a covered container and refrigerate. The oil will keep for up to 2 weeks.*

# Carmine's Bread Crumbs

*Yields about 12 cups*

1 pound sliced white bread, chopped in a food processor

2³/₄ cups grated Romano cheese

1 cup chopped garlic

1 tablespoon dried oregano

¹/₂ cup chopped fresh flat-leaf parsley

¹/₄ teaspoon cracked black pepper

There is no place for ordinary bread crumbs in Italian cooking. That's why we have our own version that we use as breading to top baked pasta dishes and other house specialties—anywhere a soft bread-crumb topping is called for.

*Combine the ingredients in a large bowl and toss thoroughly to incorporate. These bread crumbs are best used the same day, but will last up to 3 days if refrigerated.*

# Herbed Aioli

*Yields 1 cup*

2 pasteurized egg yolks

1 tablespoon minced garlic

1 teaspoon kosher salt

1/8 teaspoon cracked black pepper

1/8 teaspoon cayenne pepper

1 cup olive oil

2 teaspoons fresh lemon juice

1/2 teaspoon lemon zest

2 tablespoons chopped fresh flat-leaf parsley leaves

2 tablespoons chopped fresh basil

2 teaspoons pepperoncini brine

Aioli is a mayonnaise substitute, but it is to mayonnaise as gold is to iron, similar but unequal. Our version elevates the idea of aioli to an even higher plane, adding a wealth of spices that make it a rich, savory symphony. Although the steps are simple, you'll need to be precise and careful throughout the process. Your diligence will be more than rewarded.

*1. In the bowl of a food processor, combine the egg yolks, garlic, salt, black pepper, and cayenne and blend until smooth. With the food processor running, slowly add the oil in a steady stream until all of the oil is incorporated. Add the lemon juice to thin out the mixture as you are adding the oil. The mixture should have the consistency of mayonnaise.*

*2. Fold in the remaining ingredients and refrigerate to let the mixture cool and set up. The aioli will keep for 10 days refrigerated.*

# Toasted Bread Crumbs

*Yields 1 ½ cups*

4 slices white bread, crusts removed

4 teaspoons olive oil

1 teaspoon chopped garlic

2 tablespoons grated Romano cheese

3 teaspoons chopped fresh
flat-leaf parsley

There is simply no reason to settle for store-bought bread crumbs when making your own is so simple, quick, and rewarding. With a hint of cheese, some simple spices, and a nice toasted crunch, these are the perfect topping for a salad and great on pasta of all kinds.

*1. Dry the bread on a cooling rack, uncovered, overnight. Pulse the dried bread in a food processor until chopped into fine crumbs.*

*2. Preheat a large sauté pan over medium-high heat. Add the olive oil and garlic and sauté until the garlic is lightly browned.*

*3. Add the bread crumbs, reduce the heat to medium, and sauté until the crumbs take on an even brown color; do not burn. Toss the bread crumbs frequently; the process should take about 10 minutes.*

*4. Transfer the bread crumbs to a plate and let cool. When the crumbs are at room temperature, combine them in a bowl with the cheese and parsley and toss to mix. Store in a tightly covered container in a cool, dry place until ready to use. They will keep for about a week.*

# Garlic Butter

*Yields 4 cups*

2 pounds (8 sticks) unsalted butter, softened

1 tablespoon dried oregano

3 tablespoons garlic powder

1 teaspoon onion powder

$1/3$ cup grated Romano cheese

3 tablespoons chopped fresh flat-leaf parsley

$1/4$ cup chopped garlic

1 tablespoon kosher salt

$1/2$ teaspoon cracked black pepper

Simple garlic butter comes in handy in many different savory recipes. It's also a good spread on its own, and you can serve it with some crusty country bread, to complement the main course of your next meal.

*In the bowl of a stand mixer, combine the ingredients and blend on low. Once all the ingredients are incorporated, blend on high for 1 minute more. Transfer to a covered container and refrigerate until needed. Garlic butter will keep in the refrigerator for two weeks.*

# Brown Sauce

*Yields 4 ½ cups*

4 tablespoons (½ stick) unsalted butter

½ cup finely diced celery

½ cup finely diced carrots

½ cup finely diced white onions

½ teaspoon fresh thyme leaves

½ teaspoon kosher salt

⅛ teaspoon cracked black pepper

¼ cup all-purpose flour

6 cups beef stock

A sturdy brown sauce is the base of many great meat dishes and soups, and ours makes the most of garden-fresh ingredients and quality spices. This is a rich yet simple version that gives many of Carmine's classics ample body and an extra boost of flavor.

*1. Heat the butter in a 2-quart or larger pot over medium-high heat. Add the celery, carrots, and onion and sauté until nicely browned, 7 to 10 minutes.*

*2. Add the thyme leaves, salt, and pepper and sauté for 1 minute more. Add the flour to make a roux, and stir until absorbed. Reduce the heat to medium and cook for 3 to 4 minutes, being careful not to burn the roux.*

*3. Whisk in the stock and bring to a boil. Reduce the heat slightly and cook for 15 to 20 minutes, or until the sauce thickens.*

*4. Strain the sauce into another container and discard the vegetables. Let cool at room temperature, then refrigerate the sauce covered. The sauce will keep in the refrigerator for 2 weeks.*

# Carmine's Marinara Sauce

*Yields 10 cups*

¾ cup olive oil

¾ cup thinly sliced garlic

½ cup chopped fresh flat-leaf parsley

1 cup chopped fresh basil

Four 28-ounce cans whole, peeled San Marzano tomatoes

1 tablespoon kosher salt

½ teaspoon cracked black pepper

1 cup grated Romano cheese

Italian's call this *sugo di pomodoro,* but however you choose to say it, a basic, homemade marinara sauce is essential if you want to cook Italian regularly. The tomato-driven sauce is the foundation for many of our most popular dishes. For the home cook, it is a quick sauce for a weeknight pasta. Word to the wise, however: you'll find that San Marzano tomatoes are a bit more expensive, but don't be tempted to cut corners. The taste of these tomatoes is unrivaled, and key to making an unforgettable marinara.

*1. Heat the olive oil in a 5-quart (or larger) pot over medium-high heat. Add the garlic and cook until it browns, being careful not to let the garlic burn.*

*2. Add the parsley and the basil and cook for 1 minute. Add the tomatoes, salt, and pepper and bring to a boil. Reduce to a simmer and break up the tomatoes slightly with a wooden spoon. Cook for about 1 hour and 15 minutes, or until the sauce thickens.*

*3. Remove from the heat and fold in the cheese. You can use the marinara immediately, or refrigerate it for up to 2 weeks before using. If storing the sauce for later use, don't fold the cheese in until you're ready to use it.*

# Roasted Red Peppers

*Yields 1 ¾ pounds*

6 red bell peppers

2 tablespoons olive oil blend (3 parts canola oil to 1 part olive oil)

1 cup Garlic-Herb Oil (page 243)

2 tablespoons julienned fresh basil

Chances are that you'll find abundant uses for this particular staple, far beyond the role it plays in any other recipes. A few peppers are a wonderful quick snack with some aged Italian cheese and country bread, and they are excellent in just about any green salad.

*1. Preheat the oven to 450°F.*

*2. Rub the peppers with the oil and spread them on a half sheet pan. Roast in the oven for 15 to 20 minutes, or until the peppers are charred on about three-quarters of their outside surfaces.*

*3. Remove the peppers from the oven and transfer to a closed paper bag for 15 minutes. Remove them from the bag and let finish cooling at room temperature.*

*4. Core, seed, and skin the peppers. Cover the cleaned peppers with the garlic-herb oil and basil and refrigerate, covered, for 24 hours. Use as desired. The peppers will keep, refrigerated, for up to 2 weeks.*

# THE ITALIAN PANTRY: PICK A PEPPER

Peppers of all kinds have long been supporting players in Italian cooking. You'll likely find a much greater variety in the verdant south where they are grown in every garden; the hottest varieties in Italy are grown and used in southern regions such as Puglia and Calabria. However, peppers have found their way into every corner of the country and into dishes in every regional cuisine.

As integrated as peppers might be with what we consider classic Italian dishes, many types are not native to Europe. The truth be known, hotter peppers and even many of their lesser cousins trace their lineage back to the New World. Spanish explorers, enamored of the flavors, imported peppers back to Spain. They naturally migrated to Italy and other parts of Europe. However, in Italy, spicy heat always takes a backseat to flavor, so the peppers used are typically milder than in other international cuisines.

Depending on the type, peppers are used fresh, dried, or pickled. Pickling can add a bit of bite to a more sedate pepper, and also preserves the vegetable for use during the winter and for transport to less fertile areas. Dried peppers are less significant in Italian cooking then they are in the food of Spain or Latin countries, but they are still used, ground, as important accents.

You'd be wise to choose peppers as a chef would: select fresh in season for the best flavor and use pickled versions sparingly, adding sweeter elements to cut the sharp tang imparted by the pickling brine. The list of peppers that follows represents the most common types used in Italian (and Italian-American) cooking. Cooks from the old country inevitably had backyard gardens where many different varietals of any given pepper might be grown. But these represent the major types you're likely to find at your local specialty market or well-stocked grocery store.

**Bell peppers:** Humble as they may be, these grocery store standards are grown all over Italy. They find their way into many different dishes, including crowd-pleasing, time-tested standards like sausage and peppers. The popularity is due to the fact that they have an alluring succulence and a delicate, light flavor when used fresh, and they take to just about any spice when cooked. They are also the perfect pepper for roasting (see our Roasted Red Peppers recipe on page 252). Roasted red peppers are traditionally used in soups, sandwiches, antipasti, and even eaten all by themselves (or, for the braver soul, as a quick snack with anchovies and splash of extra-virgin olive oil). Bell peppers also make a heartwarming comfort food dish when filled with a simple stuffing of sausage, bread crumbs, mozzarella or provolone, Italian spices, and olive oil.

Any bell peppers you buy should be firm, with a shiny skin free of blemishes, soft spots, or wrinkles. Red and green bell peppers start out the same color—green is just the color of the immature pepper, and red the color of the ripe, sweeter fruit. Other colors are different varieties altogether, but will be as sweet as a red bell pepper. Red, yellow, and orange bell peppers will keep, refrigerated, for about 5 days, while green peppers will keep for a week.

**Peperoncini:** The uniquely Italian name actually describes several peppers in the *capsicum annuum* family. In Italy, the peppers can actually be quite hot; but those grown or sold in jars in America are inevitably mild. All are yellow or yellow-green and slightly bitter. They are most widely available pickled and jarred. The briny delicacies make wonderful additions to large and varied meat and cheese antipasto platters. You can also add them whole or sliced to salads and sandwiches such as heroes, or serve on the side of just about any dish as a succulent garnish. Just keep in mind that eaten whole, they tend to provide a squirt of briny pickling juice with the first bite. You can lessen the tang of the pickling vinegar's acidity by rinsing the pepper in cold water before serving.

**Cherry peppers:** Named for their plump shape, these peppers come in both hot and sweet varieties. Although they can be used in cooking like any other pepper, they are most often pickled and jarred. The brining liquid is why these are sometimes referred to, and sold in jars labeled as, "vinegar peppers." Pickled cherry peppers are often stuffed for a simple antipasto. One of the easiest ways to use them is to remove the stem and clean the peppers, wrap a small chunk of burrata or provolone with prosciutto, and stuff it in the pepper. A drizzle of olive oil and you have the ideal, quick-and-easy meal starter. Fresh cherry peppers can also be cleaned, stuffed, and baked as a warm antipasto, or sliced, sautéed, and added to pastas, sauces, or other dishes. Simplest of all, the pickled peppers are often used straight out of the jar as contrast to a selection of Italian meats and cheeses on a large cold antipasto platter.

**Italian sweet pepper:** Despite the name, these are often the hottest of Italian peppers, although still not very hot. The peppers, like bell peppers, are green when young, and red when mature. Shaped like a wind sock, the peppers are ideal for stuffing and roasting as delectable antipasti. The flavors of this pepper really come out when sautéed, which is why they are sometimes called "frying peppers." Try sautéing sliced Italian peppers as a wonderful topping for chicken, steak, or veal chops, or as an addition to a marinara or a meat sauce.

# Carmine's Menu Suggestions

Carmine's was founded on the belief that food is food, but great Italian food shared with people you care about in a warm and welcoming environment is a celebration. Wouldn't it be great if every meal could be a celebration? Well actually, it can.

It's all about combining recipes in thoughtful and creative ways. The menus and individual dishes don't necessarily have to be complex or numerous to hit the mark. In fact, you don't want to make a meal so much work that the host can't enjoy the guests, even if the "guests" are just the spouse and kids on a weeknight.

Any combination of courses in a meal—whether it's two, four, or six—must also contain a bit of magic. The dishes must work together and perfectly complement each other so that the meal is much more than the sum of its parts. That's where the creativity of putting together a menu really comes into play. We know that better than anyone, because Carmine's has been developing menus worthy of celebration for decades.

So we've put together this collection of menus to make things a little easier for peo-

ple at home. You can use these as is for super-successful meals, or change things up a little bit to suit your guests or yourself. Don't like seafood? Swap a fish dish for something meatier. Wrestling with a big sweet tooth? Add a dessert as necessary. The point is, these menus are at least great starting points. We've given them straightforward titles so you'll see at a glance the idea behind the menu, but you can take it from there and riff on the theme.

Keep in mind that it's all about fun. You're not just trying to put together ingredients, or individual dishes, you're trying to put together a celebration.

## THE COCKTAIL PARTY

*A mix of antipasti makes for perfect party platters that put canapés to shame. We've included both hot and cold recipes to add interest, adding a blend of different textures and flavors that are sure to satisfy whatever craving your party guests might have. And because your guests are as likely to be standing or walking around as they are to be sitting, these can easily be eaten with the fingers and a napkin or two.*

Cubanelle Peppers Stuffed with
Three Cheeses (page 38)
Crostini with Cannellini Bean Dip
(page 22)
Classic Arancini with Prosciutto and
Peas (page 60)
Stuffed Zucchini (page 59)
Stuffed Mushrooms (page 64)
WINE SUGGESTION: Sparkling Prosecco,
sparkling Lambrusco, a dry Rosato
(aka Rosé), Gavi or Pinot Nero.

## THE GAME DAY SPREAD

*One of the truly wonderful things about Italian food is that it can go casual just as easily as it goes fine dining. Whether your sport is baseball, hockey, football, or even European futbol, this collection of snacks will elevate the event, making any game championship caliber. Leave the guacamole and tortilla chips in the kitchen, and give your guests something extra to celebrate—win, lose, or draw!*

Artichoke Dip with Mushrooms and
Arugula (page 49)
Pizza Rustica (page 52)
Stromboli with Pepperoni and
Cheese (page 56)
Mozzarella en Carozza (page 63)
Stuffed Mushrooms (page 64)
Scarpariello Chicken Wings (page 66)
BEER SUGGESTION: Peroni lager, Moretti
La Rossa (brown nutty)
WINE SUGGESTION: Primitivo (red)

## THE WEEKDAY SPECIAL

*Just because it's Wednesday, doesn't mean you can't have a lovely, simple, and satisfying sit-down meal with your family. In fact, at Carmine's, we'd argue that a weeknight is the perfect time to do a modestly elegant meal that slows everyone down and alleviates a little bit of the stress of the midweek hustle and bustle. These dishes are simple to make and can be mostly made ahead of time, so the focus is on everyone enjoying the meal.*

Endive, Arugula, and Radicchio with
Romano Cheese (page 85)
Spaghetti with Carmine's Meatballs
(page 116)
Chocolate Torta (page 212)
WINE SUGGESTION: Barbera

## BUON COMPLEANNO!

*Holidays aside, the celebration of celebrations is a family birthday. The way to make a relative or friend feel special—and okay with another year passing by—is to create a custom meal for him or her. Bright flavors, comforting textures, and a dessert beloved by kids and adults alike are sure to put any presents on the table to shame.*

Sea Scallops Wrapped with Pancetta (page
46)
Asparagus and Fava Bean Salad with Blue
Crab (page 81)
Lamb Bolognese with Fresh Ricotta (page
122)

Titanic Ice Cream Sundae (page 215)
WINE SUGGESTION: Fiano or Chardonnay, Valpolicella Ripasso or Amarone

## THE SIT-DOWN DINNER PARTY

*There's nothing quite like the enjoyment of close friends and family gathered around a well-set table to enjoy each other's company over the course of an evening. Great food is the centerpiece of a social get-together and can make or break a dinner party. That's why we like to go fancy, with recipes that look and taste like they took way more work than they did.*

Grilled Shrimp with Fennel (page 32)
Arugula Salad with Gorgonzola (page 83)
Roasted Filet of Beef with Cipollini Onion Sauce (page 171)
Italian-Style Cheesecake (page 224)
WINE SUGGESTION: Soave or Vernaccia, Negro Amaro, Super Tuscan or Brunello

## DATE NIGHT

*Any Italian will tell you: Italian food is the stuff of* amore. *The right meal can create a romantic evening to remember. The trick is to include decadent dishes that tell the person you're cooking for you really care enough to set the best on the table.*

Hearts of Romaine with Prosciutto and Ricotta Salata (page 89)
Garlic-Roasted Broccoli (page 198)
Broiled Lobster Oreganata (page 138)
Mini Chocolate Cannoli (page 208)
WINE SUGGESTION: Franciacorte, Ferrari sparkling wine, or Prosecco

## SUMMERTIME SOIREE

*Special summer meals can happen any day of the week, but they are best eaten al fresco—outside with the last of the day's sunshine smiling over the table. The dishes themselves should capture the essence of summer, with light and bright flavors and seasonal ingredients.*

Cured Salmon with Lemon Mascarpone (page 26)
Orzo and Fresh Tuna Salad (page 35)
Roasted Eggplant Dip (page 40)
Farfalle with Chicken, Asparagus, and Mushrooms (page 102)
Escarole, Pancetta, and Cannellini Beans (page 190)
Semifreddo with Strawberries (page 228)
WINE SUGGESTION: Falaghina, Rosato (dry Rosé) or Dolcetto

# Acknowledgments

Carmine's founder Artie Cutler loved a good celebration. He enjoyed the pace, ambience, fun, and plain gusto of restaurants, and that made him a legend among New York City restaurateurs. He started not only Carmine's, but other New York City institutions including Murray's Sturgeon Shop, Dock's Oyster Bar & Seafood Grill, Haru, Ollie's Noodle Shops, Columbia and Times Square Bagels, and Monsoon. Sadly, Artie has left us. We're poorer for the loss, but his legacy stands in the spirit of celebration that goes on in every Carmine's dining room, every night of the week.

So in a sense, the idea of this book comes from Artie.

Artie's wife, Alice, tends the flame of celebration in Artie's stead, and does an amazing job. Alice keeps a steady hand on the business and is not only a wonderful leader, but a wonderful person and dear friend.

The excellence begins with Alice, but goes all the way through our organization. As CEO, I'm fortunate to have a talented, dedicated staff that helps keep Carmine's (and our other restaurants) in front of the pack in an incredibly competitive marketplace. The captain of a ship doesn't steer it alone, and

I'm grateful for all the professionals at the Alicart Restaurant Group and at Carmine's. I'm thankful for every member of the staff who contributed to this book. They've done a tremendous job. I want to tell you more about a few key contributors.

Corporate Director of Culinary Operations Glenn Rolnick led the charge on this book. Glenn serves as the eyes and the ears of all our restaurants. His dedication to quality and his passion for good food make him the best restaurant executive anyone could ask for. I consider him part of the gang of three, helping Alice and me grow the company and keeping Carmine's the wonderful place it is. I thank both my wife and Glenn's wife—the two Karens—for their patience, tolerance, and support. Their love and resilience—especially through new restaurant openings and demanding special projects such as this book—have allowed us to grow in new and exciting directions.

I'd also like to give a big tip of the hat to our talented Corporate Executive Chef Neal Corman. He is a real trouper and talent in the kitchen. Glenn and Neal carefully tested, retested, revised, and perfected the recipes in this book, making each dish as good as it could possibly be (and as easy for the home cook as possible).

The following people were also crucial to the book's success. Beverage Director Erin Ward has a passion for Italian wines that comes through in all the wine information and recommendations in this book. Her contributions helped make this book more of a Carmine's experience.

Thanks to the Carmine's in Times Square, NYC General Manager Mario Contacessi and Chef Louis Javier; Carmine's 91st Street General Manager James Yacyshyn and Chef Joe Delgado; Carmine's at the Tropicana in Atlantic City General Manager Valeri McLaughlin and Chef Jeff Gotta; The team at Carmine's D.C.; Carmine's Las Vegas General Manager Andy Hooper and Chef Michael Ingino; Carmine's at the Atlantis in the Bahamas General Manager LeTroy Lowe and Chef Claudio Infanti; Alicart Executive Director of Operations Randy Talbot; Carmine's Director of Human Resources Espi Criscuolo; Marketing Manager Jennifer Wolinski; Director of Training Genny Gomez; Director of Banquets Penny Kaplan, and Director of Off-Premise Catering John Dancu.

Leading our accounting staff at Alicart is Drew Kuruc, along with Teresa Chang, Franz Steele, and their team. A special thanks to Jennifer Roth, who was often the glue that held the project together.

Agents Jane Dystel and Miriam Goderich knocked themselves out to get this book sold and see it come to life, and for that we will be eternally grateful. This book would not have become a reality without St. Martin's Press and the vast experience and expertise of Elizabeth Beier, as well as her indomitable assistants Michelle Richter and Anya Lichtenstein.

Thanks also to Alex Martinez, whose pictures bring to life so many of the classic Carmine's recipes and provide a sense of the magic that is Carmine's dining room. Thanks to Jeremy Deutsch and the rest of the guys at Deutsch, Metz & Deutsch. Additional thanks to Roy Tumpowsky, one of our trusted advisors, and to Dr. Jane Sullivan, of Sullivan and Associates, whose advice has always been insightful and valuable.

Last, but of course not least, thanks to Jody and Danielle Cutler, and Sarah and Andrew Bank, because family is everything.

—Jeffrey Bank
New York City, 2014

# Index

Salata, *88,* 89

Prosecco, 14

Protected Designation of
  Origin (POD), 82

Provolone cheese, 51

pure olive oil, 23

R

radicchio, 85

rice, 140–41

Riserva, 15

risotto, 140–41

Roasted Eggplant Dip, 40

Roasted Filet of Beef with
  Cipollini Onion Sauce,
  171–72, *173,* 174

Roasted Garlic, 242

Roasted Red Peppers, 252, *253*

Roasted Tomatoes, 172

Roasted Vegetables, 202, *203*

Robiola cheese, 51

Rolled Beef with Hot Cherry
  Peppers, 28, *29*

Roma tomatoes, 186–87

Roman Catholic Church, 126

Romano and Black Pepper
  Bread Sticks, 41

rosemary, fresh, 157
  Crusty Rosemary Potatoes,
    *200,* 201

S

saffron, 157

sage, 157

Sagrantino, 12

salads

Arugula Salad with
  Gorgonzola, 83

Asparagus and Fava Bean
  Salad with Blue Crab,
  *80,* 81

Carmine's House Salad Mix,
  69–70, 72

Endive, Arugula, and
  Radicchio with Romano
  Cheese, 85

Hearts of Romaine with
  Prosciutto and Ricotta
  Salata, *88,* 89

Mesclun Greens with
  Grilled Vegetables, 78, *79*

Mixed Olive Salad, 86, *87*

Orzo and Fresh Tuna Salad,
  *34,* 35

Seafood Salad, 90–91

Spinach and Bocconcini
  Salad, 84

Tuscan Bean Salad, *76,* 77

salmon

Cured Salmon with Lemon
  Mascarpone, 26–27, *27*

Stuffed Salmon, 134–35, *135*

salt, Kosher, 156

Sambuca, 210

San Marzano tomatoes, 186–87

sauces, 148–49, *149,* 152–53

Beef Involtini, 177–78, *179*

Brown Sauce, 249

Carmine's Marinara, 251

Porterhouse Pizzaiola,
  161–62

Rack of Lamb, 168, *169,* 170

Roasted Filet of Beef with
  Cipollini Onion Sauce,
  171–72, *173,* 174

sausage, 167

Chicken Sausage with
  Broccoli Rabe, 58

Orecchiette with Sausage
  and Broccoli Rabe, 96, *97*

Sausage, Peppers, Potatoes,
  and Onions, 164–65, *165*

Sautéed Spinach, 195

scallops, 47

Scallops and Shrimp
  Scarpariello, *142,* 143

Sea Scallops Wrapped in
  Pancetta, 46

Scarpariello Chicken Wings,
  66–67, *67*

Sea Bass Cioppino, 128–29, *129*

seafood. *See also* fish and
  seafood
  Seafood Salad, 90–91

*secondo. See* main dishes

Semifreddo with Strawberries,
  228–29, *229*

shallots, 175

shellfish, 127. *See also* fish and
  seafood

shrimp

Grilled Shrimp with Fennel,
  *32, 33*

Scallops and Shrimp
  Scarpariello, *142,* 143

Shrimp alla Roma, 106–7,
  *107*

side dishes *(contorni), 180,*